THE ULTIMATE
COLLECTION OF

crochet
edgings™

Annie's

All edgings and projects are made with Brown Sheep Cotton Fleece yarn.

Annie's® *The Ultimate Collection of Crochet Edgings* is published by Annie's, 306 East Parr Road, Berne, IN 46711. Printed in USA. Copyright © 2016 Annie's. All rights reserved. This publication may not be reproduced in part or in whole without written permission from the publisher.

RETAIL STORES: If you would like to carry this publication or any other Annie's publication, visit AnniesWSL.com.

Every effort has been made to ensure that the instructions in this publication are complete and accurate. We cannot, however, take responsibility for human error, typographical mistakes or variations in individual work. Please visit AnniesCustomerService.com to check for pattern updates.

Library of Congress Control Number: 2016935881   ISBN: 978-1-59012-659-2   1 2 3 4 5 6 7 8 9

CONTENTS

Popular crochet designer Belinda "Bendy" Carter has created the ultimate edging book, an essential guide that no creative crocheter will want to be without!

Now you can turn what has often been an afterthought in crochet design, the edging, into a "pièce de résistance", the perfect finishing touch to any crocheted item.

No matter if you are a beginner or a seasoned pro, whether you prefer traditional designs or cutting-edge fashion, you are sure to find just what you are looking for in this incredible book.

With *The Ultimate Collection of Crochet Edgings* as a guide, you can take your creativity to new heights! Written in a clear, easy-to-follow style, and filled with beautiful, full-color photographs, this book is sure to become an indispensable reference guide you will find yourself turning to time and time again.

You will find an exciting variety of unique and unusual edgings in this stunning book, including lace, floral, ribs, beads, ruffles, sculpture, fringe and points plus eight original designs ranging from a fabulous lace coat to an amazing knit-look dishcloth.

So grab your crochet hook and take your crochet designs where they've never gone before!

General Information
Edgings
Work a row of single crochet or slip stitches evenly spaced across top or bottom of edgings that are worked from side to side, if desired, for a more finished look.

Some edgings are worked from top to bottom or bottom to top.

Most edgings begin by working in back bar of chain (*see illustration*) for a smoother bottom edge.

Back Bar of Chain

Beading Needle
Make 4-inch beading needle to string beads: Cut an 8-inch piece of waxed dental floss, hold the ends of the floss together forming a loop (eye), insert end of yarn through the loop in the floss so that about 3 inches of the yarn is through the loop, squeeze the ends of the floss together so that they stick together, forming point of needle.

lace

CHAPTER ONE

pineapple fans

SPECIAL STITCHES

Beginning shell (beg shell): Ch 3 *(counts as first dc)*, (dc, ch 2, 2 dc) in same ch-2 sp.

Shell: (2 dc, ch 2, 2 dc) in next ch-2 sp.

Double shell: (2 dc, {ch 2, 2 dc} twice) in next ch-2 sp.

Row 1 (RS): Ch a multiple of 12 sts plus 2, sc in **back bar** *(see illustration on page 4)* of 2nd ch from hook and in back bar of each ch across, turn.

Row 2: Ch 3 *(counts as first dc)*, (dc, ch 2, 2 dc) in same st, [sk next 5 sts, (dc, ch 2, dc) in next st, sk next 5 sts, (2 dc, ch 2, 2 dc) in next st] across, turn.

Row 3: Sl st in each of first 2 sts, sl st in next ch sp, **beg shell** *(see Special Stitches)*, [ch 1, 6 dc in next ch-2 sp, ch 1, **shell** *(see Special Stitches)*] across, turn.

Row 4: Sl st in each of first 2 sts, sl st in next ch sp, beg shell, *sk next 2 sts, [ch 1, dc in next dc] 6 times, sk next 2 dc, ch 1, shell, rep from * across, turn.

Row 5: Sl st across to ch sp, beg shell, *ch 1, sk next ch-1 sp, sc in next ch-1 sp, [ch 3, sc in next ch-1 sp] 4 times, ch 1, sk next ch-1 sp**, **double shell** *(see Special Stitches)*, rep from * across, ending last rep at **, shell, turn.

First Pineapple Top

Row 1 (WS): Sl st across to ch sp, beg shell, ch 1, sk next ch-1 sp, sc in next ch-3 sp, [ch 3, sc in next ch-3 sp] 3 times, ch 1, sk next ch-1 sp, shell, leaving rem sts unworked, turn.

Row 2: Sl st across to ch sp, beg shell, ch 1, sk next ch-1 sp, sc in next ch-3 sp, [ch 3, sc in next ch-3 sp] twice, ch 1, sk next ch-1 sp, shell, turn.

Row 3: Sl st across to ch sp, beg shell, ch 1, sk next ch-1 sp, sc in next ch-3 sp, ch 3, sc in next ch-3 sp, ch 1, sk next ch-1 sp, shell, turn.

Row 4: Sl st across to ch sp, beg shell, ch 1, sk next ch-1 sp, sc in next ch-3 sp, ch 1, sk next ch-1 sp, shell, turn.

Row 5: Sl st across to ch sp, ch 3, **dc dec** *(see Stitch Guide)* in same ch sp and next ch sp, dc in same ch sp. Fasten off.

Next Pineapple Top

Row 1 (WS): Join with sl st in next unworked ch sp on row 5 of Lace, beg shell, ch 1, sk next ch-1 sp, sc in next ch-3 sp, [ch 3, sc in next ch-3 sp] 3 times, ch 1, sk next ch-1 sp, shell, leaving rem sts unworked, turn.

Rows 2–5: Rep rows 2–5 of First Pineapple Top.

Rep Next Pineapple Top across.

lace

lacy fans

Row 1 (RS): Ch a multiple of 8 sts plus 2, sc in **back bar** *(see illustration on page 4)* in 2nd ch from hook and in back bar of each ch across, turn.

Row 2: Ch 1, sc in first st, [ch 3, sk next 3 sts, sc in next st] across, turn.

Row 3: Ch 1, sc in first st, [ch 1, sk next ch sp, (dc, ch 1) 5 times in next st, sk next ch sp, sc in next st] across, turn.

Row 4: Ch 1, sc in first st, ch 3, sk next ch-1 sp, sc in next ch-1 sp, *[ch 3, sc in next ch-1 sp] 3 times**, ch 2, sk next 2 ch-1 sps, sc in next ch-1 sp, rep from * across, ending last rep at **, ch 3, sk next ch-1 sp, sc in last st. Fasten off.

twisted broomstick lace

Row 1 (RS): Ch a multiple of 5 plus 1, sc in **back bar** *(see illustration on page 4)* of 2nd ch from hook, sc in back bar of each ch across, **do not turn**.

Row 2 (RS): Slip lp on hook on broomstick, [working from left to right, insert hook in next st, yo, pull through, slip lp on broomstick *(see Fig. 1)* across, do not turn.

Row 3: *Insert crochet hook from left to right through lps on broomstick, slip 5 lps on hook *(see Fig. 2)*, yo, pull through all 5 lps, ch 1, (sc, {ch 1, sc} twice) in same 5-lp group *(see Fig. 3)*, rep from * across. Fasten off.

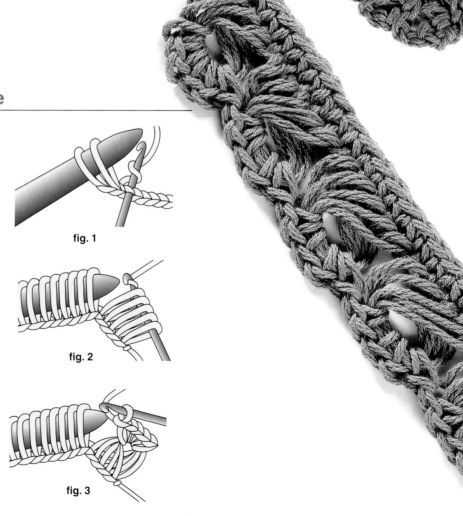

fig. 1

fig. 2

fig. 3

Broomstick Lace

2-loop broomstick lace

Row 1 (RS): Ch a multiple of 2 plus 1, sc in **back bar** *(see illustration on page 4)* of 2nd ch from hook, sc in back bar of each ch across, **do not turn.**

Row 2 (RS): Slip lp on hook on broomstick, [working from left to right, insert hook in next st, yo, pull through, slip lp on broomstick *(see Fig. 4)* across, **do not turn.**

fig. 4

Brookmstick Lace

Row 3: *Insert crochet hook from left to right through lps on broomstick, slip 2 lps on hook, yo, pull through all 2 lps, ch 1, (sc, ch 3, sc) in same 2-lp group, rep from * across. Fasten off.

wavy broomstick lace

PATTERN NOTE

Various sizes of knitting needles may be used for broomstick.

Row 1 (RS): Ch a multiple of 4 plus 2, sc in **back bar** *(see illustration on page 4)* of 2nd ch from hook, sc in back bar of each ch across, **do not turn.**

Row 2 (RS): Slip lp on hook on broomstick, *working from left to right, ◊insert hook in next st, yo, pull through, slip lp on medium-size broomstick◊ *(see Fig. 4)*, insert hook in next st, yo, pull up through, slip lp on small broomstick, rep between ◊ once, insert hook in next st, yo, pull through, slip lp on broomstick, rep from * across, **do not turn.**

Row 3: Carefully pull lps off hooks, maintaining lp height, insert hook through first lp, yo, pull through, ch 1, sc in lp, [ch 1, sc in next lp] across. Fasten off.

lace

classic broomstick lace

Row 1 (RS): Ch a multiple of 3 plus 2, sc in **back bar** *(see illustration on page 4)* of 2nd ch from hook, sc in back bar of each ch across, **do not turn**.

Row 2 (RS): Slip lp on hook on **broomstick** *(see Fig. 4)*, *working from left to right, insert hook in **back lp** *(see Stitch Guide)* of next st, yo, pull lp through, slip lp on broomstick, insert hook in **front lp** *(see Stitch Guide)* of same st, yo, pull lp through, slip lp on broomstick, rep from * across to last st, insert hook through both lps of last st, yo, pull through, slip lp on broomstick, **do not turn**.

Row 3: *Insert hook from left to right through 6 lps*, yo, pull through all lps*, ch 1, 3 sc in center of all lps, ch 1, [insert hook from left to right through 6 lps, yo, pull through all lps on hook, ch 1, 2 sc in center of all lps, ch 1] across to last 6 lps, rep between *, 3 sc in center of lps. Fasten off.

fig. 4

Brookmstick Lace

picot lace

SPECIAL STITCH

Picot: Sl st in indicated st, ch 2, sl st in back bar of 2nd ch from hook, sl st in same st as beg sl st.

Row 1 (RS): Ch in multiple of 4 sts plus 1, sc in **back bar** *(see illustration on page 4)* of 2nd ch from hook and in back bar of each ch across, turn.

Row 2: Ch 5, sk first 3 sts, [**picot** *(see Special Stitch)* in next st, ch 5, sk next 3 sts] across to last st, sl st in last st, turn.

Row 3: Ch 5, [picot in center of ch-5 sp, ch 5] across to last ch-5 sp, sl st in center of last ch-5 sp, turn.

Next row: Rep row 3 until piece is 1 row less than desired length.

Last row: [Ch 4, sl st in 2nd ch from hook, ch 2, picot in ch-5 sp] across. Fasten off.

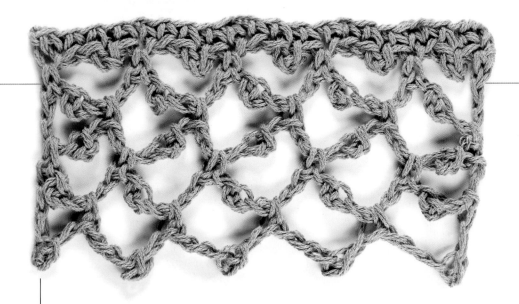

irish lace

SPECIAL STITCH

Picot: Sl st in back bar of 2nd ch from hook.

Row 1 (RS): Ch in multiple of 4 sts plus 2, sc in **back bar** *(see illustration on page 4)* of 2nd ch from hook, [sc in back bar of each of next 2 chs, ch 2, **picot** *(see Special Stitch)*, sc in back bar in each of next 2 chs] across, turn.

Row 2: Ch 1, sc in first st, [ch 5, picot, ch 1, sc in ch sp to the left of picot] across, turn.

Next rows: Rep row 3 until piece is desired length. At end of last row, fasten off.

cross-stitch

Row 1 (RS): Ch in multiple of 2 sts plus 1, sc in **back bar** *(see illustration on page 4)* of 2nd ch from hook and in each ch across, turn.

Row 2: Ch 1, sc in each st across, turn.

Row 3: Ch 2 *(counts as first hdc)*, [sk next st, dc in next st, working in back of dc just made, dc in sk st] across to last st, hdc in last st. Fasten off.

lace

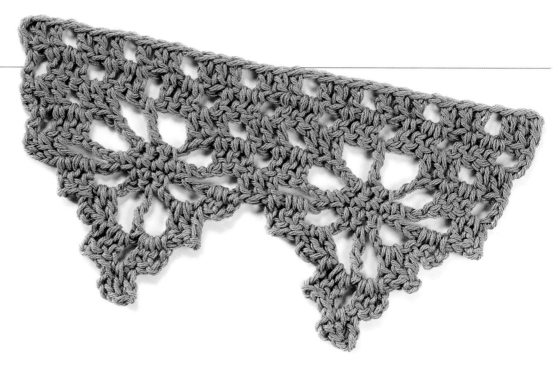

diamond points

SPECIAL STITCHES
Mesh: Ch 1, sk next st or ch, dc in next st or ch.
Block: [Dc in next ch or st] twice.

Row 1 (RS): Ch a multiple of 16 plus 5, dc in **back bar** *(see illustration on page 4)* of 4th ch from hook, dc in back bar of next ch, working in back bars, [**mesh** *(see Special Stitches)*, **block** *(see Special Stitches)*] across, turn.

Row 2: Ch 3, [mesh, block] across to last 2 sts, mesh, turn.

Row 3: Ch 3, [block, mesh, block, ch 3, sk next 2 sts, tr in next ch sp, ch 3, sk next 2 sts, dc in next st, block, mesh] across to last 2 sts, block, turn.

Row 4: Ch 3, [mesh, block, ch 4, sk next 2 dc, sc in next ch-3 sp, sc in next tr, sc in next ch-3 sp, ch 4, sk next 2 dc, dc in next dc, block] across to last 2 sts, mesh, turn.

Row 5: Ch 3, [block, ch 4, sk next 2 sts, sc in next ch-4 sp, sc in each of next 3 sc, sc in next ch-4 sp, sk next 2 dc, dc in next dc] across to last 2 sts, mesh, turn.

First Diamond Top

Row 1: Sl st in each of first 3 sts, ch 3, block in ch-4 sp, ch 3, sk next sc, sc in each of next 3 sc, ch 3, sk next sc, block in next ch-4 sp, dc in next dc, leaving rem sts unworked, turn.

Row 2: Sl st in each of first 3 dc, ch 3, block in ch-3 sp, ch 2, sk next sc, tr in next sc, ch 2, sk next sc, block in next ch-3 sp, dc in next dc, leaving rem sts unworked, turn.

Row 3: Sl st in each of first 3 dc, ch 3, block in next ch-2 sp, ch 1, sk next tr, block in next ch-2 sp, dc in next dc, leaving rem sts unworked, turn.

Row 4: Sl st in each of first 3 dc, ch 3, block, leaving rem sts unworked. Fasten off.

Next Diamond Top

Row 1: Sk next dc on row 5 of Lace, join with sl st in next st, ch 3, block in next ch-4 sp, ch 3, sk next sc, sc in each of next 3 sc, ch 3, sk next sc, block in next ch-4 sp, dc in next dc, leaving rem sts unworked, turn.

Rows 2–4: Rep rows 2–4 of First Diamond Top.

Rep Next Diamond Top across.

medallions

SPECIAL STITCHES

Double treble decrease (dtr dec): Sk next 2 ch-3 sps on same Medallion, holding back last lp of each st on hook, dtr in next ch-3 sp on same Medallion and in corresponding ch-3 sp on next Medallion, yo, pull through all lps on hook.

End decrease (end dec): Yo twice, insert hook around st 2 rows below, yo, pull through, [yo, pull through 2 lps on hook] twice, insert hook in last st on Edging, yo, pull through all lps on hook.

Lace

Note: Design is worked on a multiple of 12 sts plus 11.

Medallion

Make 1 Medallion for every multiple of 12 sts on edging plus 1 more Medallion.

Rnd 1: Ch 4, sl st in first ch to form ring, sl st in ring, ch 4 *(counts as dc and ch-1)*, [dc in ring, ch 1] 11 times, join with sl st in 3rd ch of beg ch-4.

Rnd 2: Ch 1, sc in first st, ch 3, [sc in next st, ch 3] 11 times, join with sl st in beg sc. Fasten off.

Edging

Row 1 (RS): Join with sl st in ch-3 sp on first Medallion, ch 9 *(counts as first dtr and ch-4)*, sk next 2 ch-3 sps on same Medallion, sc in next ch-3 sp, *ch 5, **dtr dec** *(see Special Stitches)*, ch 5, sk next 2 ch-3 sps on same Medallion as last st, sc in next ch-3 sp, rep from * until all Medallions are used, ch 4, sk next 2 ch-3 sps on same Medallion, dtr in next ch-3 sp, turn.

Row 2: Ch 1, sc in each st and in **back bar** *(see illustration on page 4)* of each ch across, turn.

Row 3: Ch 1, **fptr** *(see Stitch Guide)* around post of dtr 2 rows below, sc in each of next 4 sts, [fptr around next sc 2 rows below, sc in each of next 5 sts, fptr around next dtr 2 rows below, sc in each of next 5 sts] across to last 6 sts, fptr around next sc 2 rows below, sc in each of next 4 sts, **end dec** *(see Special Stitches)*. Fasten off.

lace

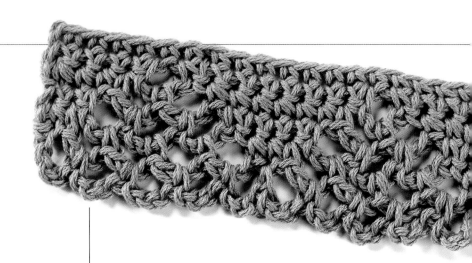

broken lace

Row 1 (RS): Ch in multiple of 9 sts plus 2, sc in **back bar** *(see illustration on page 4)* of 2nd ch from hook and in each ch across, turn.

Row 2: Ch 1, sc in first st, [sc in each of next 4 sts, ch 3, sc in each of next 5 sts] across, turn.

Row 3: Ch 1, sc in first st, [sc in each of next 3 sts, ch 3, sk next st sc in next ch-3 sp, ch 3, sk next st, sc in each of next 4 sts] across, turn.

Row 4: Ch 1, sc in first st, [sc in each of next 2 sts, ch 3, sk next st, sc in next ch-3 sp, ch 3, sk next st, sc in next ch-3 sp, ch 3, sk next st, sc in each of next 3 sts] across, turn.

Row 5: Ch 1, sc in first st, *sc in next st, ch 3, sk next st, sc in next ch-3 sp, [ch 3, sc in next ch-3 sp] twice, ch 3, sk next st, sc in each of next 2 sts, rep from * across, turn.

Row 6: Ch 1, sc in first st, *ch 3, sk next st, sc in next ch-3 sp, [ch 3, sc in next ch-3 sp] 3 times, ch 3, sk next st, sc in next st, rep from * across. Fasten off.

lacy filet

Row 1 (RS): Ch in multiple of 2 sts plus 2, sc in **back bar** *(see illustration on page 4)* of 2nd ch from hook and in each ch across, turn.

Row 2: Ch 3 *(counts as first hdc and ch-1 sp)*, sk next st, hdc in next st, [ch 1, sk next st, hdc in next st] across. Fasten off.

simple pineapple

Lace

Row 1 (RS): Ch multiple of 9 plus 1, sc in **back bar** *(see illustration see page 4)* of 2nd ch from hook, sc in back bar of each ch across, turn.

Row 2: Ch 1, sc in each st across, turn. Fasten off.

First Pineapple

Row 1: With RS facing, sk first 4 sts, join with sl st in next st, ch 3, 5 dc in same st, leaving rem sts unworked, turn.

Row 2: Ch 4 *(counts as first dc and ch-1 sp)*, dc in next st, [ch 1, dc in next st] 4 times, turn.

Row 3: Ch 1, sk first st, sc in next ch-1 sp, [ch 3, sc in next ch-1 sp] 4 times, turn.

Row 4: Ch 1, sk first st, sc in next ch-3 sp, [ch 3, sc in next ch-3 sp] 3 times, turn.

Row 5: Ch 1, sk first st, sc in next ch-3 sp, [ch 3, sc in next ch-3 sp] twice, turn.

Row 6: Ch 1, sk first st, sc in next ch-3 sp, ch 3, sc in next ch-3 sp. Fasten off.

Next Pineapple

Row 1: Sk next 8 sts on Lace, join with sl st in next st, ch 3, 5 dc in same st, leaving rem sts unworked, turn.

Rows 2–6: Rep rows 2–6 of First Pineapple.

Rep Next Pineapple across to Last Pineapple.

Last Pineapple

Row 1: Sk next 8 sts on Lace, join with sl st in next st, ch 3, 5 dc in same st, leaving rem sts unworked, turn.

Rows 2–5: Rep rows 2–5 of First Pineapple.

Row 6: Ch 1, sk first st, sc in next ch-3 sp, ch 3, sc in next ch-3 sp, leaving last 4 sts on Lace unworked. Fasten off.

Edging

With RS facing, join with sl st in first st on Lace, *sl st in each st across to Pineapple, sl st in end of first row, evenly sp [sl st, ch 1] 22 times around Pineapple, sl st in next st on Lace, rep from * across to last 3 sts, sl st in each of last 3 sts. Fasten off.

lace

lacy lavender coat

SKILL LEVEL

INTERMEDIATE

FINISHED SIZES

Instructions given fit 32–34-inch bust *(small)*; changes for 36–38-inch bust *(medium)* 40–42-inch bust *(large)* and 44–46-inch bust *(X-large)* are in [ ].

FINISHED GARMENT MEASUREMENTS

Bust: 40 inches *(small)* [44 inches *(medium)*, 48 inches *(large)*, 52 inches *(X-large)*]

MATERIALS

- Brown Sheep Co. Cotton Fleece light (light worsted) weight yarn (3½ oz/215 yds/ 99g per skein):
    8 [9, 10, 10] skeins CW800 prairie lupine
- Size H/8/5mm crochet hook or size needed to obtain gauge
- Tapestry needle
- 1-inch flower buttons #1202 by LaMode: 4

GAUGE

24 sts = 6 inches; 20 rows = 6 inches
Take time to check gauge.

PATTERN NOTES

When working increase or decrease rows, always begin and end row with single crochet.

Work increases and decreases on wrong-side rows only.

Coat is designed to be knee length, but due to the weight of this yarn the coat will be longer when worn.

INSTRUCTIONS

COAT

Back

Row 1 (WS): Ch 106 [114, 122, 130], sc in **back bar** *(see illustration on page 4)* of 2nd ch from hook, [ch 3, sk next 3 chs, sc in back bar of next ch] across, turn. *(105 [113, 121, 129] sc and chs)*

Row 2 (RS): Ch 1, sc in first st, [ch 1, with hook in front of ch-3 sp, dc in back bar of 2nd ch of 3 sk chs, ch 1, sc in next st] across, turn.

Row 3: Ch 1, sc in first st, ch 1, sk next ch-1 sp, sc in next dc, [ch 3, sk next 2 ch-1 sps and next st, sc in next dc] across to last 2 sts, ch 1, sk next ch-1 sp, sc in last st, turn.

Row 4: Ch 1, sc in first st, ch 1, sk next ch-1 sp, sc in next sc, [ch 1, with hook in front of ch-3 sp, dc in sk sc 2 rows below, ch 1, sc in next sc]

across to last 2 sts, ch 1, sk next ch-1 sp, sc in last st, turn.

Row 5: Ch 1, sc in first st, *ch 3, sk next 2 ch sps and next sc**, sc in next dc, rep from * across to last st, ending last rep at **, sc in last st, turn.

Row 6: Ch 1, sc in first st, [ch 1, with hook in front of ch-3 sp, dc in sk sc 2 rows below, ch 1, sc in next sc] across, turn.

Rows 7–18: Rep rows 3–6 consecutively for pattern.

Next rows: Continue working and

maintaining established pattern and at the same time, *[dec 1 st at each end of next row, work 3 rows even without dec] 3 times, dec 1 st at each end of next row, work 5 rows without dec, rep from * twice. *(81 [89, 97,105] sts at end of last row)*

Next rows: Continue working in established pattern for 2 more rows.

Armhole Shaping

Next row: Sl st in each of first 6 [6, 8, 8] sts, work in pattern across, leaving last 6 [6, 8, 8,] sts unworked, turn. *(69 [77, 81, 89] sts)*

Next rows: Continue working and maintaining established pattern and at the same time, [work 1 row even without dec, dec 2 sts at each end of next row] 3 [4, 4, 5] times. *(57 [61, 65, 69] sts at end of last row)*

Next rows: Continue working in established pattern for 13 [13, 15, 13] rows.

First Neck Shaping

Row 1: Work in established pattern for 17 [19, 19, 21] sts, leaving rem sts unworked, turn.

Row 2: Work in pattern across. Fasten off.

2nd Neck Shaping

Row 1: Sk next 23 [23, 27, 27] sts, join with sl st in next st, work in established pattern across, turn.

Row 2: Work in pattern across. Fasten off.

Front
Make 2.

Row 1 (WS): Ch 54 [58, 62, 66], sc in back bar of 2nd ch from hook, [ch 3, sk next 3 chs, sc in back bar of next ch] across, turn. *(53 [57, 61, 65] sc and chs)*

Row 2 (RS): Ch 1, sc in first st, [ch 1, with hook in front of ch-3 sp, dc in back bar of 2nd ch of 3 sk chs, ch 1, sc in next st] across, turn.

Rows 3–18: Rep rows 3–18 of Back.

Next rows: Continue working and maintaining established pattern and at the same time, *[dec 1 st at arm edges on next row, work 3 rows even without dec] 3 times, dec 1 st at arm edge on next row, work 5 rows even without dec, rep from * once, [dec 1 st at arm edge on next row, work 3 rows even without dec] twice, dec 1 st at arm edge on next row. *(42 [46, 50, 54] sts at end of last row)*

Next rows: Continue working in established pattern except when repeating on row 4 and on row 6, place hook in back of ch-3 sp to work dc in sk sc 2 rows below instead of placing hook in front of ch-3 sp, continue in pattern and, at the same time maintaining pattern as much as possible, work 3 rows even without dec, dec 1 st at arm edge on next row, work 7 rows without dec. *(41 [45, 49, 53] sts at end of last row)*

Armhole Shaping

Next row: Continue working and maintaining established pattern and at the same time, dec 6 [6, 8, 8] sts at arm edge on next row. *(35 [39, 41, 45] sts)*

Next rows: Continue working and maintaining established pattern and at the same time, [work 1 row even without dec, dec 2 sts at arm edge on next row] 3 [4, 4, 5] times. *(29 [31, 33, 35] sts at end of last row)*

Next rows: Continue working in established pattern for 15 [15, 17, 15] rows. At end of last row, fasten off.

Collar

With WS facing, join with sl st to front as follows:
On right front, join with sl st in 13th st from neck opening.
On left front, join with sl st in first st at neck opening.

Row 1: Ch 1, work in established pattern for 13 sts, turn.

Next rows: Continue working in established pattern for 17 [17, 19, 19] rows. At end of last row, fasten off.

Sleeve
Make 2.

Row 1 (WS): Ch 34 [34, 42, 42], sc in back bar of 2nd ch from hook, [ch 3, sk next 3 chs, sc in back bar of next ch] across, turn. *(33 [33, 41, 41] sc and chs)*

lace

Row 2 (RS): Ch 1, sc in first st, [ch 1, with hook in front of ch-3 sp, dc in back bar of 2nd ch of sk 3 chs, ch 1, sc in next st] across, turn.

Next rows: Work rows 3–6 of Back for pattern and at the same time, maintaining pattern as much as possible, inc 1 st at each end of next row, then inc 1 st at each end of every 2nd row 2 [6, 2, 6] times, then inc 1 st at each end of every 4th row 9 [7, 9, 7] times. *(57 [61, 65, 69] sts at end of last row)*

Next rows: Work in established pattern for 5 [5, 7, 7] rows.

Cap Shaping

Next row: Continue working in established pattern and at the same time, maintaining pattern as much as possible, dec 6 [6, 8, 8] sts at each end of next row. *(45 [49, 49, 53] sts)*

Next rows: Continue working in established pattern and at the same time, maintaining pattern as much as possible, [work 1 row even without dec, dec 2 sts at each end of next row] 3, [3, 2, 2] times. *(33 [37, 41, 45] sts at end of last row)*

Next rows: Work even in established pattern without dec for 1 [1, 3, 3] rows.

Next rows: Continue working in established pattern and at the same time, maintaining pattern as much as possible, [dec 4 sts at each end of next row, work 1 row even without dec] twice. At end of last row, fasten off. *(17 [21, 25, 29] sts at end of last row)*

FINISHING

1. Sew shoulder seams.

2. Fold Sleeve in half, place fold at shoulder seam and sew in place. Rep with rem Sleeve.

3. Sew side and Sleeve seams.

4. Sew last row of left Front Collar to last row of right Front collar, then sew Collar to back neck opening easing in fullness.

Bottom Lace

Row 1 (RS): With RS facing, working in starting chs on opposite side of row 1 across bottom of Fronts and Back, join with sc in first ch, [ch 1, sk next 3 chs, (dc, ch 1) 5 times in next ch, sk next 3 chs, sc in next ch] across, turn.

Row 2: Ch 1, sc in first st, ch 3, sk next ch-1 sp, sc in next ch-1 sp, *[ch 3, sc in next ch-1 sp] 3 times**, ch 2, sk next 2 ch-1 sps, sc in next ch-1 sp, rep from * across, ending last rep at **, ch 3, sk next ch-1 sp, sc in last st. Fasten off.

Sleeve Lace

Rnd 1 (RS): With RS facing, working in starting ch on opposite side of row 1, join with sc in first ch at joining, *ch 1, sk next 3 chs, (dc, ch 1) 5 times in next ch**, sk next 3 chs, sc in next ch, rep from * around, ending last rep at **, sk last 4 chs, join with sl st in beg sc, **turn.**

Rnd 2: Sl st in next ch-1 sp, sl st in dc, sl st in next ch-1 sp, ch 1, sc in same ch sp, *[ch 3, sc in next ch-1 sp] 3 times, ch 2, sk next 2 ch-1 sps**, sc in next ch-1 sp, rep from * around, ending last rep at **, join with sl st in beg sc. Fasten off.

Front & Collar Edging

Row 1: With RS facing, join with sl st at right Front opening ch-3 sp, ch 1, sc in first row on Front, *ch 1, sk end of next row, sc in end of next row, rep from * up right Front, around Collar and down left Front, ch 1, sc in next ch-3 sp, turn.

Row 2: [Ch 3, sk next ch-1 sp, sl st in next sc] across. Fasten off.

Buttons

Coat is fastened by using ch-3 sps on Edging. Using ch sps for placement, sew first button to Left Front when pattern changes from crocheting with hook in front of ch-3 sp to crocheting with hook in back of ch-3 sp, then sew on 3 more buttons going down Left Front, spacing buttons 2 inches apart.

Fold Collar back, beg at first button.

floral

violets

Background

Row 1 (RS): With A, ch any multiple of chs plus 1, sc in **back bar** *(see illustration on page 4)* of 2nd ch from hook, and in back bar of each ch across, turn.

Row 2: Ch 1, sc in each st across, turn.

Rows 3–5: Rep row 2. At end of last row, fasten off.

Violet

Make 1 for every 2 inches on Background, alternating 2 different shades of purple.

Ch 4, sl st in first ch to form ring, sl st in ring, [ch 3, dc in ring, ch 2, sl st in ring] 5 times. Fasten off. With matching color, sew Violets to Background.

With yellow, embroider French knot *(see illustration)* in center of each Violet.

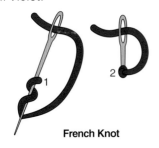

French Knot

pansies

Background

Row 1 (RS): With A, ch multiple of 10 chs plus 1, sc in **back bar** *(see illustration on page 4)* of 2nd ch from hook, and in back bar of each ch across, turn.

Row 2: Ch 1, sc in first st, [sc in **front lp** *(see Stitch Guide)* of next st, sc in **back lp** *(see Stitch Guide)* of next st] across to last st, sc in both lps of last st, turn.

Rows 3–9: Rep row 2. At end of last row, fasten off.

Pansy

Make 1 for every 10 sts on Background.

Rnd 1: With B, ch 2, (sc, ch 3) 3 times in 2nd ch from hook, join with sl st in beg sc. Fasten off. Pull beg end tight to close.

Rnd 2: Join C with sc in any ch-3 sp, (dc, 2 tr, dc, sc) in same ch sp, (sc, dc, 2 tr, dc, sc) in each of next 2 ch-3 sps, do not join.

Row 3: Sk first st, [ch 3, sl st in behind petals between next 2 sc] twice, turn, **do not join**.

Row 4: [Ch 3, sl st in same sp where last sl st made on last row between petals] twice, turn.

Row 5: Working in both ch-3 sps of last 2 rows at same time, (sc, 2 dc, 3 tr, 2 dc, sc) in each of next 2 ch sps. Fasten off. Sew Pansy on Background.

floral

sunflowers

PATTERN NOTE
Change color in last stitch made.
Carry B on wrong side of work catching
it up in stitch every few stitches to
prevent dangling.

SPECIAL STITCHES
Double front post double treble (double fpdtr):
Holding back last lp of each st on hook,
2 fpdtr around indicated st 2 rows below, yo,
pull through all lps on hook. Leave st behind
fpdtr unworked.

Puff stitch (puff st): [Yo, insert hook in indicated
st, yo, pull through, yo, pull through 2 lps on
hook] 5 times, yo, pull through all lps on hook.

Background
Row 1 (RS): With A, ch multiple of 9 plus 1, sc in **back
bar** *(see illustration on page 4)* of 2nd ch from hook and
in each ch across, turn.

Row 2: Ch 1, sc in each st across, turn.

Row 3: Ch 1, sc in each of first 4 sts **changing colors**
(see Stitch Guide) to B, ***fptr** *(see Stitch Guide)* around
st 2 rows below changing to A**, sc in each of next 8
sts changing to B, rep from * across, ending last rep at
**, sc in each of last 4 sts, turn.

Row 4: Rep row 2.

Row 5: Ch 1, sc in each of first 2 sts changing to B,
***double fpdtr** *(see Special Stitches)* around fptr

2 rows below changing to A, sc in next st changing to
B, fptr around same fptr 2 rows below changing to A, sc
in next st, changing to B, double fpdtr around same fptr
2 rows below, changing to A**, sc in each of next 4 sts
changing to B, rep from * across, ending last rep at **,
sc in each of last 2 sts, turn.

Rows 6 & 7: Rep rows 2 and 3. At end of last row,
fasten off B.

Row 8: Rep row 2.

Row 9: Ch 1, sc in each of first 4 sts changing to C,
***puff st** *(see Special Stitches)* in next st changing to A,
fasten off C**, sc in each of next 8 sts changing to C,
rep from * across, ending last rep at **, sc in each of
last 4 sts, turn.

Rows 10–13: Rep row 2. At end of last row, fasten off.

Flower
Make 1 for every puff st on Background.
With D, ch 4, sl st in first ch to form ring, [sl st in ring,
ch 8] 6 times, join with sl st in beg sl st. Fasten off.
Place each Flower over a puff st, pull puff st through
center of each Flower.

slip-stitch basket

PATTERN NOTE

When working a back slip stitch or a slip stitch over back slip stitch in the previous row, the top horizontal loop will be the back loop of the stitch; when working a back slip stitch or slip stitch over a slip stitch in previous row, the top horizontal loop will be the front loop of the stitch.

SPECIAL STITCH

Back slip stitch (back sl st): Bring yarn to front of work, insert hook in indicated st from back to front so hook is facing down, yarn should be to the right of hook, move yarn to the left going over the hook then move yarn to the right going under the hook thereby catching the yarn in the hook, pull the yarn through st and the lp on the hook turning the hook counterclockwise so the hook is now facing up.

Background

Row 1 (RS): With A, ch 13, sl st in **back bar** *(see illustration on page 4)* of 2nd ch from hook, and in back bar of each of next 3 chs, **back sl st** *(see Special Stitch)* in each of next 4 chs, sl st in back bar in each of last 4 chs, turn.

Row 2: Ch 1, back sl st in **front lp** *(see Stitch Guide)* in each of first 4 sts, sl st in **back lp** *(see Stitch Guide)* in each of next 4 sts, back sl st in front lp in each of last 4 sts, turn.

Row 3: Ch 1, sl st in back lp in each of first 4 sts, back sl st in front lp in each of next 4 sts, sl st in back lp in each of last 4 sts, turn.

Rows 4 & 5: Rep rows 2 and 3.

Row 6: Rep row 2.

Row 7: Ch 1, back sl st in back lp of each of first 4 sts, sl st in front lp in each of next 4 sts, back sl st in back lp in each of last 4 sts, turn.

Row 8: Rep row 3.

Rows 9–12: Rep rows 2 and 3 alternately.

Row 13: Ch 1, sl st in front lp in each of first 4 sts, back sl st in back lp in each of next 4 sts, sl st in front lp in each of last 4 sts, turn.

Next rows: Rep rows 2–13 consecutively until desired length ending with row 6 or row 12. At end of last row, fasten off.

Finishing

1. With B and using straight st *(see illustration)*, embroider a stem and 2 leaves on every other square on Background.

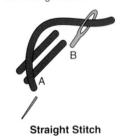

Straight Stitch

2. With C embroider French knot *(see illustration)* above each stem for miniature rose.

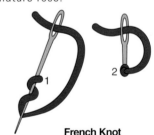

French Knot

floral

clockwise chain

SPECIAL STITCH

Chain flower: Ch 1, work around post of last sc, (sc, ch 3) 3 times around post of sc, (sc, ch 3) 3 times around post of next to last sc, join with sl st in beg sc.

Background

Row 1 (RS): Ch 7, sc in **back bar** *(see illustration on page 4)* of 2nd ch from hook, and in back bar of each ch across, turn.

Row 2: Ch 1, sc in each st across, turn.

Row 3: Ch 1, sc in each of first 4 sts, make **chain flower** *(see Special Stitch)*, sc in each of last 2 sts, turn.

Row 4: Ch 1, sc in each of first 2 sts, sc in each of next 2 sts where flower was worked in side of sts, sc in each of last 2 sts, turn. *(6 sc)*

Rows 5–8: Rep row 2.

Next rows: Rep rows 3–8 consecutively until desired length, ending with row 5. Fasten off.

looped daisy

PATTERN NOTE

Design requires a 2½-inch piece of cardboard.

SPECIAL STITCH

Loop single crochet (lpsc): Wrap yarn from front to back around cardboard, sc in next st, this will create 2½-inch lp in back of work, remove lp from cardboard.

Background

Row 1 (RS): Ch multiple of 9 chs plus 1, sc in **back bar** *(see illustration on page 4)* of 2nd ch from hook, and in back bar of each ch across, turn.

Rows 2 & 3: Ch 1, sc in each st across, turn.

Row 4: Ch 1, sc in each of first 3 sts, *lpsc *(see Special Stitch)* in each of next 3 sts*, sc in each of next 6 sts, rep from * across, ending last rep at **, sc in each of last 3 sts, turn.

Rows 5 & 6: Rep rows 3 and 4.

Rows 7–9: Rep row 2. At end of last row, fasten off.

Daisy

For each Daisy section *(3 lps on bottom and 3 lps on top)*, tie top left and bottom right lp in knot, tie top right and bottom left lp in knot over last knot, [tie top center lp and bottom center lp in knot over last knot] twice.

lily of the valley

SPECIAL STITCH

Surface stitch (surface st): Holding yarn at back of work, insert hook in sp between sts, yo, pull lp through sp and lp on hook.

Background

Row 1 (RS): With A, ch 14, sc in **back bar** *(see illustration on page 4)* of 2nd ch from hook, and in back bar of each ch across, turn.

Row 2: Ch 1, sc in first st, [sc in **front lp** *(see Stitch Guide)* of next st, sc in **back lp** *(see Stitch Guide)* of next st] 5 times, sc in front lp of next st, sc in both lps of last st, turn.

Next rows: Rep row 2 to desired length, working a multiple of 18 rows plus 1. At end of last row, fasten off.

Stems

With B, work **surface st** *(see Special Stitch)* on Background as shown on chart.

Lily of the Valley

Make 6 for every 18 rows on Background.

Rnd 1: With C, ch 2, 5 sc in 2nd ch from hook, **do not join**. *(5 sc)*

Rnds 2 & 3: Sc in each st around.

Rnd 4: [Sc in next st, ch 2, sl st in 2nd ch from hook] around, join with sl st in beg sc. Fasten off. Sew each Lily of the Valley to Background according to chart.

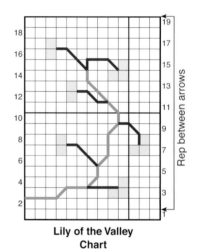

**Lily of the Valley
Chart**

STITCH KEY
- ▨ Surface st worked over same sts twice
- ■ Surface st worked once
- ☐ Lily of the Valley placement

floral

berry cluster

PATTERN NOTES

Leave stitches behind post
  stitches unworked.
Post stitches are worked around
  post of stitches 2 rows
  below throughout.

SPECIAL STITCHES

Berry stitch (berry st): (Ch 1,
6 dc, ch 1) as indicated.

**Closing berry stitch (closing
berry st):** Yo, insert hook through
first and last ch-1 sps on berry
st, yo, pull lp through, [yo, pull
through 2 lps on hook] twice, sk
st behind closing berry st.

**Front post treble crochet
decrease (fptr dec):** Holding back
last lp of each st on hook, fptr
around next closing berry st, fptr
around fptr below, fptr around
post of st 2 sts to left, yo, pull
through all lps on hook.

Background

Row 1 (RS): Ch multiple of 11 chs
plus 1, sc in **back bar** *(see
illustration on page 4)* of 2nd ch from
hook, and in back bar of each ch
across, turn.

Rows 2 & 3: Ch 1, sc in each st
across, turn.

Row 4: Ch 1, sc in each of first 5 sts,
ch 1, sk next st**, sc in each of next
10 sts, rep from * across, ending last
rep at **, sc in each of last
5 sts, turn.

Row 5: Ch 1, sc in each of first
5 sts, *sk next ch-1 sp, **berry st**
(see Special Stitches) in sk st 2 rows
below keep ch-1 in back of work**,
sc in each of next 10 sts, rep from *
across, ending last rep at **, sc in
each of last 5 sts, turn.

Row 6: Ch 1, sc in each of first 2 sts,
ch 1, sk next st, sc in each of next 2
sts, [sk berry st, sc in next sk ch-1 sp
2 rows below, sc in each of next 2
sts, ch 1, sk next st, sc in each of
next 2 sts] across, turn.

Row 7: Ch 1, sc in each of first 2
sts, sk next ch-1 sp, berry st in sk
st 2 rows below keeping ch-1 sp in
back of work, sc in each of next 2
sts, [**closing berry st** *(see Special
Stitches)*, sc in each of next 2 sts, sk
next ch-1 sp, berry st in sk st 2 rows
below keeping ch-1 sp in back of
work, sc in each of next 2 sts]
across, turn.

Row 8: Ch 1, sc in each of first
2 sts, [sk berry st, sc in next ch-1 sp
2 rows below, sc in each of next
5 sts, sk berry st, sc in next ch-1 sp
2 rows below, sc in each of next
2 sts] across, turn.

Row 9: Ch 1, sc in each of first 3 sts,
*closing berry st, sc in next st, **fptr**
(see Stitch Guide) around st 2 rows
below, sc in next st, closing berry
st**, sc in each of next 6 sts, rep
from * across, ending last rep at **,
sc in each of last 3 sts, turn.

Row 10: Rep row 2.

Row 11: Ch 1, sc in each of first
5 sts, ***fptr dec** *(see Special
Stitches)***, sc in each of next 10 sts,
rep from * across, ending last rep at
**, sc in each of last 5 sts, turn.

Row 12: Rep row 2.

Row 13: Ch 1, sc in each of first
5 sts, *fptr around fptr dec below**,
sc in each of next 10 sts, rep from *
across, ending last rep at **, sc in
each of last 5 sts. Fasten off.
Open berries by pushing top of
berries down.

butterfly & leaves

SPECIAL STITCHES

Double front post double treble (double fpdtr): Holding back last lp of each st on hook, 2 fpdtr around indicated st 2 rows below, yo, pull through all lps on hook. Leave st behind fpdtr unworked.

Double back post triple treble (double bptrtr): Holding back last lp of each st on hook, 2 bptrtr around indicated st 2 rows below, yo, pull through all lps on hook. Leave st behind bptrtr unworked.

Background

Row 1 (RS): Ch multiple of 16 plus 3, sc in **back bar** *(see illustration on page 4)* of 2nd ch from hook and in each ch across, turn.

Row 2: Ch 1, sc in each st across, turn.

Row 3: Ch 1, sc in each of first 13 sts, *fptr *(see Stitch Guide)* around st 2 rows below**, sc in each of next 15 sts, rep from * across, ending last rep at **, sc in each of last 4 sts, turn.

Row 4: Rep row 2.

Row 5: Ch 1, sc in each of first 4 sts, *double fpdtr *(see Special Stitches)* around st 2 sts to right 2 rows below, sc in next st, double fpdtr around post of st 2 sts to left, sc in each of next 4 sts, double fpdtr around fptr, sc in next st, fptr around same fptr below**, sc in each of next 6 sts, rep from * across, ending last rep at **, sc in each of last 4 sts, turn.

Row 6: Rep row 2.

Row 7: Ch 1, sc in each of first 5 sts, *yo twice, insert hook around posts of both double post sts below, yo, pull lp through, yo twice, insert hook around post of st 4 rows below, yo, pull lp through, [yo, pull through 2 lps on hook] 6 times, sc in each of next 7 sts, fptr around fptr below, sc in next st, double fpdtr around same fptr**, sc in each of next 5 sts, rep from * across, ending last rep at **, sc in each of last 2 sts, turn.

Row 8: Ch 1, sc in each of first 9 sts, *double bptrtr *(see Special Stitches)* around post of double post st 3 rows below and 2 sts to left, sc in each of next 5 sts, double bptrtr around post of double post st 3 rows below and 2 sts to right**, sc in each of next 9 sts, rep from * across, ending last rep at **, sc in each of last 2 sts, turn.

Row 9: Ch 1, sc in each of first 11 sts, *double fpdtr round post of st 2 sts to left**, sc in each of next 15 sts, rep from * across, ending last rep at **, sc in each of last 6 sts, turn.

Row 10: Rep row 2. Fasten off.

floral

leaf cluster

PATTERN NOTES

Leave stitches behind post
  stitches unworked.
Post stitches are worked around
  stitches 2 rows below throughout.
Change colors in last stitch made.

SPECIAL STITCH

**Front post double treble crochet
(fpdtr):** Yo 3 times, insert hook
around post of st 2 rows below,
yo, pull through st, yo, complete
as dtr.

Background

Row 1 (RS): With A, ch multiple of
19 chs plus 1, sc in **back bar** *(see
illustration on page 4)* of 2nd ch from
hook, and in back bar of each ch
across, turn.

Row 2: Ch 1, sc each st across, turn.

Row 3: Ch 1, sc in each of first 10 sts
changing colors *(see Stitch Guide)* to
B, ***fptr** (see Stitch Guide)* around post
of st 2 rows below, changing to A**,
sc in each of next 16 sts, rep from *
across, ending last rep at **,
sc in each of last 8 sts, turn.

Row 4: Rep row 2.

Row 5: Ch 1, sc in each of first 9 sts
changing colors to B, fptr around fptr
below, changing to A, sc in each of
next 2 sc, changing to B, ***fpdtr** (see
Special Stitch)* around same fptr
below, changing to A**, sc in each
of next 15 sts, rep from * across,

ending last rep at **, sc in each of
last 6 sts, turn.

Row 6: Rep row 2.

Row 7: Ch 1, sc in each of first
7 sts changing colors to B, *fpdtr
around fpdtr below, changing to A,
sc in next st, changing to B, fptr
around same fpdtr changing to A**,
sc in each of next 16 sts, rep from *
across, ending last rep at **, sc in
each of last 9 sts, turn.

Row 8: Rep row 2.

Row 9: Ch 1, sc in each of first 8 sts
changing colors to B,*fptr around fptr
below, changing to A, sc in each of
next 2 sts, changing to B, fpdtr around
same fptr changing to A**, sc in each
of next 15 sts, rep from * across,
ending last rep at **, sc in each of
last 7 sts, turn.

Row 10: Rep row 2.

Row 11: Ch 1, sc in each of first 6 sts
changing to B, *fpdtr around fptr
below changing to A, sc in next st
changing to B, fptr around same fptr
changing to A**, sc in each of next

16 sts, rep from * across, ending
last rep at **, sc in each of last
10 sts, turn.

Row 12: Rep row 2.

Row 13: Ch 1, sc in each of first
7 sts changing to B, *fptr around fptr
changing to A**, sc in each of next 18
sts, rep from * across, ending last rep
at **, sc in each of last 11 sts, turn.

Rows 14–20: Rep row 2. At end of
last row, fasten off.

Leaf

**Make 5 Leaves for every 19 sts on
Background.**

With B, ch 7, sc in back bar of 2nd ch
from hook, work in back bar of chs,
hdc in next ch, dc in each of next
2 chs hdc in next ch, sc in next ch,
ch 1, working on opposite side of
ch, working in **back lps** *(see Stitch
Guide)*, sc in next ch, hdc in next ch,
dc in each of next 2 chs, hdc in next
ch, sc in last ch. Fasten off.
Sew Leaves to Background as shown
in photo.

daylilies

Background

Row 1 (RS): With A, ch multiple of 18 chs plus 1, sc in **back bar** *(see illustration on page 4)* of 2nd ch from hook, and in back bar of each ch across, turn.

Row 2: Ch 1, sc in first st, [sc in **front lp** *(see Stitch Guide)* of next st, sc in **back lp** *(see Stitch Guide)* of next st] across with sc in both lps of last st, turn.

Rows 3–15: Rep row 2. At end of last row, fasten off.

Stamens

Rnd 1: With B, ch 3, sl st in first ch to form ring, ch 1, 6 sc in ring, **do not join**. *(6 sc)*

Rnd 2: [Sl st in next st, pull up 3-inch lp, turn hook clockwise 10 times to twist, sl st in last sl st] 6 times, join with sl st in beg sl st. Fasten off.

Bottom Petals

Rnd 1: Join C with sc in any sc on rnd 1 of Stamens, [ch 2, sk next st, sc in next st] twice, ch 2, sk next st, join with sl st in beg sc.

First Petal

Row 2: Now working in rows, sl st in first ch-2 sp, ch 3 *(counts as first dc)*, 5 dc in same ch sp, leaving rem sts unworked, turn.

Row 3: Ch 2 *(does not count as first st)*, dc in next st, dc in each of next 2 sts, **dc dec** *(see Stitch Guide)* in last 2 sts, turn. *(4 dc)*

Row 3: Ch 2, dc in next st, dc dec in last 2 sts. Fasten off.

Next Petal

Row 1: Join C with sl st in next ch-2 sp, ch 3, 5 dc in same ch sp, leaving rem sts unworked, turn.

Rows 2 & 4: Rep rows 2 and 4 of First Petal.
Rep Next Petal once.

Top Petals

Rnd 1: With D, leaving long end at beg, ch 6, sl st in first ch to form ring, ch 1, sc in ring, ch 2, [sc in ring, ch 2] twice, join with sl st in beg sc.

First Petal

Rows 1–4: Rep rows 1–4 of First Petal on Bottom Petals.

Next Petal

Rows 1–4: With D, rep rows 1–4 of Next Petal on Bottom Petals.
Rep Next Petal once.

Assembly

1. Weave long end of Top Petals in and out of ch-2 sps, pull Stamens through ch-6 ring, then pull long end tight to close.

2. Place Bottom Petals on Background, place Top Petals on top of Bottom Petals as shown in photo, sew in place.

floral

nature's garden pullover

SKILL LEVEL
INTERMEDIATE

FINISHED SIZES

Instructions given fit 32–34-inch bust
(small); changes for 36–38-inch bust
(medium) 40–42-inch bust *(large)* and
44–46-inch bust *(X-large)* are in [ ].

FINISHED GARMENT MEASUREMENTS

Bust: 36 inches *(small)* [40 inches
(medium), 45 inches *(large)*,
50 inches *(X-large)*]

MATERIALS

- Brown Sheep Co. Cotton
  Fleece light (light worsted)
  weight yarn (3½ oz/215 yds/99g
  per skein):

    4 [5, 5, 6] skeins CW380 dusty sage
- Size H/8/5mm crochet hook or size
  needed to obtain gauge
- Tapestry needle
- Stitch markers

GAUGE

10 sts = 3 inches; 22 rows = 7 inches
Take time to check gauge.

PATTERN NOTES

Post stitches are worked around post of stitches 2 rows below unless otherwise indicated.

Leave stitches behind post stitches unworked.

To maintain established front loop/back loop pattern, work front loop single crochet in back loop single crochet of previous row and work back loop single crochet in front loop single crochet of previous row.

Always begin and end rows with single crochet in both loops.

SPECIAL STITCHES

Double front post double treble (double fpdtr): Holding back last lp of each st on hook, 2 fpdtr around indicated st 2 rows below, yo, pull through all lps on hook. Leave st behind fpdtr unworked.

Double back post triple treble (double bptrtr): Yo 4 times, insert hook around post of indicated st from back of work, yo, pull lp through, [yo, pull through 2 lps on hook] 4 times, yo 4 times, insert hook around post of same st, yo, pull lp through, [yo, pull through 2 lps on hook] 4 times, yo, pull through all lps on hook.

Surface stitch (surface st): Holding yarn at back of work, insert hook in sp between sts, yo, pull lp through sp and lp on hook.

INSTRUCTIONS

LADY'S TOP
Back

Row 1: Ch 60 [68, 76, 84], sc in **back bar** (see illustration on page 4) of 2nd ch from hook and in back bar of each ch across, turn. (59 [67, 75, 83] sc)

Row 2: Ch 1, sc in each st across, turn.

Row 3: Ch 1, sc in each of first 13 [15, 13, 14] sts, *fptr around next st 2 rows below, sc in each of next 15 [17, 15, 17] sts, rep from * 1 [1, 2, 2] times, fptr around next st, sc in each of last 13 [15, 13, 14] sts, turn.

Row 4: Rep row 2.

Row 5: Ch 1, sc in each of first 4 [5, 4, 4] sts, ***double fpdtr** (see Special Stitches) around post of st 2 sts to right, sc in next st, double fpdtr around post of st 2 sts to left, sc in each of next 4 [5, 4, 5] sts, double fpdtr around post of fptr 2 sts to left, sc in next st, fptr around same post st as last double fpdtr, sc in each of next 6 [7, 6, 7] sts, rep from * 2 [2, 3, 3] times, double fpdtr around post of st 2 sts to right, sc in next st, double fpdtr around post of st 2 sts to left, sc in each of last 4 [5, 4, 4] sts, turn.

Row 6: Rep row 2.

Row 7: Ch 1, sc in each of first 5 [6, 5, 5] sts, ◊*yo twice, insert hook around post of both double post sts below, yo, pull lp through, yo twice, insert hook around post of st 4 rows below, yo, pull lp through, [yo, pull through 2 lps on hook] 6 times*, sc in each of next 7 [8, 7, 8] sts, fptr around post of fptr, sc in next st, double fpdtr around same post st as last post st, sc in each of next 5 [6, 5, 6] sts, rep from ◊ 2 [2, 3, 3] times, rep between * once, sc in each of last 5 [6, 5, 5] sts, turn.

Row 8: Ch 1, sc in each of first 2 [3, 2, 2] sts, ◊***double bptrtr** (see Special Stitches) around post of double post st 3 rows below and 2 sts to left, sc in each of next 5 sts, double bptrtr around post of double post st 3 rows below and 2 sts to right*, sc in each of next 9 [11, 9, 11] sts, rep from ◊ 2 [2, 4, 4] times, rep between * once, sc in each of last 2 [3, 2, 2] sts, turn.

Row 9: Ch 1, sc in each of first 11 [13, 11, 12] sts, ◊*double fpdtr around fptr 2 sts to left*, sc in each of next 15 [17, 15, 17] sts, rep from ◊ 1 [1, 2, 2] times, rep between * once, sc in each of last 15 [17, 15, 16] sts, turn.

Row 10: Rep row 2.

Row 11 (RS): Ch 1, sc in first st, [sc in **front lp** (see Stitch Guide) of next st, sc in **back lp** (see Stitch Guide) of next st] across to last 2 sts, sc in front lp of next st, sc in both lps of last st, turn.

Row 12 (WS): Ch 1, sc in first st, [sc in back lp of next st, sc in front lp of next st] across to last 2 sts, sc in back lp of next st, sc in both lps of last st, turn.

floral

Next rows: Rep rows 11 and 12 alternately for pattern until piece measures 12 [12, 13, 13] inches from beg, ending with row 11.

Armhole Shaping
Next row (WS): Sl st in each of first 6 sts, ch 1, sc in same st as sl st, [sc in front lp of next st, sc in back lp of next st] across to last 7 sts, sc in front lp of next st, sc in both lps of next st, leaving rem sts unworked, turn. *(49 [57, 65, 73] sts)*

Next rows: Continue in established pattern and at the same time dec 1 [1, 2, 2] sts at each end of next row, then dec 1 [1, 2, 2] sts at each end of every other row till there are 43 [47, 49, 53] sts on last row.

Next rows: Continue working established pattern until 20 [22, 24, 24] rows have been completed from beg of Armhole Shaping.

First Neck Shaping
Row 1 (WS): Work in established pattern across first 11 [12, 13, 14] sts, leaving rem sts unworked, turn.
Row 2: Work in pattern across. Fasten off.

2nd Neck Shaping
Row 1 (WS): Sk next 21 [23, 23, 25] st, join with sc in next st, work in established pattern across, turn.
Row 2: Rep row 2 of First Neck Shaping.

Front
Work same as Back to Armhole Shaping.

Armhole Shaping
Next row (WS): Sl st in each of first 6 sts, ch 1, sc in same st, [sc in front lp of next st, sc in back lp of next st] 15 [17, 19, 22] times, mark last st

worked, [sc in front lp of next st, sc in back lp of next st] 5 times, mark last st worked, [sc in front lp of next st, sc in back lp of next st] 3 [5, 7, 8] times, sc in front lp of next st, sc in both lps of next st, leaving rem sts unworked turn. Move markers up with each row.

Next rows: Shape armhole opening on Front to match armhole opening on Back and at the same time, when 3 [5, 7, 7] rows from beg armhole shaping have been completed, work Butterfly on front as follows for the next 10 rows, work in established pattern to marked st, insert Butterfly row from marked st to marked st. *(11 sts)* Work in pattern across to end of row;
Butterfly row 1 (RS): Work sc in front lp of next st, sc in back lp of next st, sc in front lp of next st, sc in each of next 5 sts, sc in front lp of next st, sc in back lp of next st, sc in front lp of next st.

Butterfly row 2 (WS): Sc in back lp of next st, sc in each of next 9 sts, sc in back lp of next st.

Butterfly row 3 (RS): Sc in front lp next st, sc in each of next 9 sts, sc in front lp of next st.

Butterfly row 4: Sc in both lps of each of next 11 sts.

Butterfly row 5: Sc in each of next 4 sts, double fpdtr around post of st 2 sts to right 2 rows below, sc in next st, double fpdtr around post st 2 sts to left 2 rows below, sc in each of next 4 sts.

Butterfly row 6: Sc in each of next 11 sts.

Butterfly row 7: Sc in each of next 5 sc, yo twice, insert hook around posts of both double post sts below, yo, pull lp through, yo twice, insert hook around post of st 4 rows below, yo, pull lp through, [yo, pull through 2 lps on hook] 6 times, sc in each of next 5 sts.

Butterfly row 8: Sc in back lp of next st, sc in both lps of next st, double bptrtr around post of double post st 3 rows below and 2 sts to left, sc in each of next 5 sts, double bptrtr around post of double post st 3 rows below and 2 st to right, sc in both lps of next st, sc in back lp of next st.

Butterfly row 9: Rep Butterfly row 3.

Butterfly row 10: Sc in back lp of next st, sc in front lp of next st, sc in back lp of next st, sc in both lps of each of next 5 sts, sc in back lp

of next st, sc in front lp of next st, sc in back lp of next st; Butterfly completed.

Next rows: Work 2 rows even in established pattern.

First Neck Shaping

Next row: Work in established pattern across first 15 [16, 17, 18] sts, leaving rem sts unworked, turn.

Next rows: Work in established pattern for 4 more rows dec 1 st at neck edge on every row. *(11 [12, 13, 14] sc at end of last row)*

Next rows: Work even in established pattern for 2 rows. At end of last row, fasten off.

2nd Neck Shaping

Row 1 (WS): Sk next 13 [15, 15, 17] sts, join with sc in next st, work in established pattern across, turn.

Row 2: Rep row 2 of First Neck Shaping.

Sleeve
Make 2.

Row 1: Ch 36 [40, 44, 48], sc in back bar of 2nd ch from hook and in each ch across, turn. *(35 [39, 43, 47] sc)*

Row 2: Ch 1, sc in each st across, turn.

Row 3: Sc in first st, 2 sc in next st, sc in each of next 5 [5, 7, 7] sts, *2 sc in next st, sc in each of next 2 [3, 3, 4] sts, fptr around next st, sc in each of next 2 sts, 2 sc in next st*, sc in each of next 7 [8, 8, 9] sts, rep

between * once, sc in each of next 5 [6, 8, 9] sts, 2 sc in next st, sc in last st, turn. *(41 [45, 49, 53] sts)*

Row 4: Rep row 2.

Row 5: Ch 1, sc in each of first 3 [3, 5, 5] sts, *double fpdtr around post of st 2 sts to right, sc in next st, double fpdtr around post of st 2 sts to left**, sc in each of next 4 [5, 5, 6] sts, double fpdtr around post of fptr 2 sts to left, sc in next st, fptr around same post st as last double fpdtr, sc in each of next 6 [7, 7, 8] sts, rep from * once, rep from * to ** once, sc in each of last 3 [3, 5, 5] sts, turn.

Row 6: Rep row 2.

Row 7: Ch 1, sc in each of first 4 [4, 6, 6] sc, ◊*yo twice, insert hook around posts of both double post sts below, yo, pull lp through, yo twice, insert hook around post of st 4 rows below, yo, pull lp through, [yo, pull through 2 lps on hook] 6 times*, sc in each of next 7 [8, 8, 9] sts, fptr around post of next fptr, sc in next st, double fpdtr around post of same as last fpdtr, sc in each of next 5 [6, 6,7] times, rep from ◊ once, rep between * once, sc in each of last 4 [4, 6, 6] sts, turn.

Row 8: Ch 1, sc in first 1 [1, 3, 3] sts, ◊*double bptrtr around post of double post st 3 rows below and 2 sts to left, sc in each of next 5 sts, double bptrtr around post of double post st 3 rows below and 2 sts to right*, sc in each of next 9 [11, 11, 13] sts, rep from ◊ once, rep between *, sc in last 1 [1, 3, 3] sts, turn.

floral

Row 9: Ch 1, sc in each of first 10 [11, 13, 14] sts, *double fpdtr around fptr of st 2 sts to left*, sc in each of next 15 [17, 17, 19] sts, rep between * once, sc in each of last 14 [15, 17, 18] sts, turn.

Row 10: Rep row 2.

Row 11: Ch 1, sc in first st, [sc in front lp of next st, sc in back lp of next st] across to last 2 sts, sc in front lp of next st, sc in both lps of last st, turn.

Row 12: Ch 1, sc in first st, [sc in back lp of next st, sc in front lp of next st] across to last 2 sts, sc in back lp of next st, sc in both lps of last st, turn.

Cap Shaping

Next row: Sl st in each of first 6 sts, ch 1, sc in same st, [sc in back lp of next st, sc in front lp of next st] across to last 7 sts, sc in back lp of next st, sc in both lps of next st, leaving rem sts unworked, turn. *(31 [35, 39, 43] sts)*

Next rows: Working Cap Shaping in established pattern dec 1 st at each end of next row then dec 1 st at each end of every other row until there are *(27 [29, 33, 35] sts)*.

Next rows: Work even in established pattern for 6 [4, 5, 3] rows without dec.

Next rows: Work in pattern 4 rows dec 2 sts at each end of every other row. At end of last row, fasten off. *(11 [13, 17, 19] sts at end of last row)*

FINISHING

1. Sew shoulder seams.

2. Fold Sleeve in half, place fold at shoulder seam, sew in place. Rep with rem Sleeve.

3. Sew side and Sleeve seams.

Neck Edging

Rnd 1: With RS facing, join with sc at seam, evenly sp sc around, join with sl st in beg sc.

Rnd 2: Sl st in each st around, join with sl st in beg sl st. Fasten off.

TRIM

1. With RS facing, join with sl st to row 10 at seam on Back, **surface st** *(see Special Stitches)* around, join with sl st in beg st. Fasten off.

2. With RS facing, working in starting ch on opposite side of row 1 on Sleeve, join with sl st in first st, sl st in each st around, join with sl st in beg sl st. Fasten off. Rep on rem Sleeve.

3. With RS facing, join with sl st in row 10 at seam on Sleeve, surface st around, join with sl st in beg sl st. Fasten off. Rep on rem Sleeve.

4. With RS facing, surface st a circle around Butterfly on the Front, working surface sts around the sc on background of Butterfly, join with sl st in beg st. Fasten off.

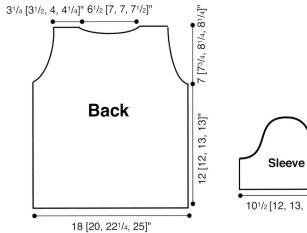

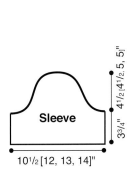

ribs

CHAPTER THREE

twisted rib

PATTERN NOTES

Leave stitches behind post stitches
  unworked.

Post stitches are worked around post
  of stitches 2 rows below throughout.

SPECIAL STITCH

Front post double treble cross-stitch (fpdtr cross-st): Sk next
2 sts 2 rows below, fpdtr in next
st on this row, sc in next st, with
hook in front of post st just made,
fpdtr in first sk st 2 rows below.

Background

Row 1 (RS): Ch multiple of 4 chs plus
2, sc in **back bar** *(see illustration on
page 4)* of 2nd ch from hook, and in
back bar of each ch across, turn.

Row 2: Ch 1, sc in each st
across, turn.

Row 3: Ch 1, sc in first st, [**fpdtr
cross-st** *(see Special Stitch)*, sc in
next st] across, turn.

Next rows: Rep rows 2 and 3 to
desired length. At end of last row,
fasten off.

stacked clusters

SPECIAL STITCH

Cluster (cl): Holding back last lp of each st on hook,
  3 dc as indicated, yo, pull through all lps on hook.

Background

Row 1 (RS): Ch multiple of 3 chs plus 1, sc in **back bar**
(see illustration on page 4) of 2nd ch from hook, and in
back bar of each ch across, turn.

Row 2: Ch 1, sc in first st, *cl *(see Special Stitch)* in
next st**, sc in next 2 sts, rep from * across, ending last
rep at **, sc in last st, turn.

Row 3: Ch 1, sc in first st, *sl st in next st**, sc in each
of next 2 sts, rep from * across, ending last rep at **, sc
in last st, turn.

Next rows: Rep rows 2 and 3 to desired length, ending
with row 2. At end of last row, fasten off.

ribs

reverse single crochet rib

Background

Row 1 (RS): Ch any number of chs plus 1, sc in **back bar** *(see illustration on page 4)* of 2nd ch from hook, and in back bar of each ch across, **do not turn**.

Row 2: Work from left to right in **front lps** *(see Stitch Guide)*, **reverse sc** *(see illustration)* in each st across, do not turn.

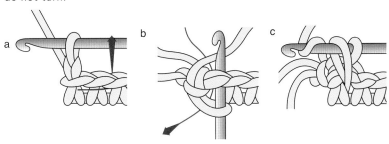

Reverse Single Crochet

Row 3: Working in **back lps** *(see Stitch Guide)* sc in each st across, do not turn.

Next rows: Rep rows 2 and 3 alternately to desired length. At end of last row, fasten off.

spike stitch rib

Background

Row 1 (RS): Ch an odd number of chs plus 1, sc in **back bar** *(see illustration on page 4)* of 2nd ch from hook, and in back bar of each ch across, turn.

Row 2: Ch 1, sc in each st across, turn.

Row 3: Ch 1, sc in first st, *insert hook in st 2 rows below, yo, pull lp through and up even with this row, yo, pull through both lps on hook, sc in next st, rep from * across, turn.

Next rows: Rep rows 2 and 3 to desired length. At end of last row, fasten off.

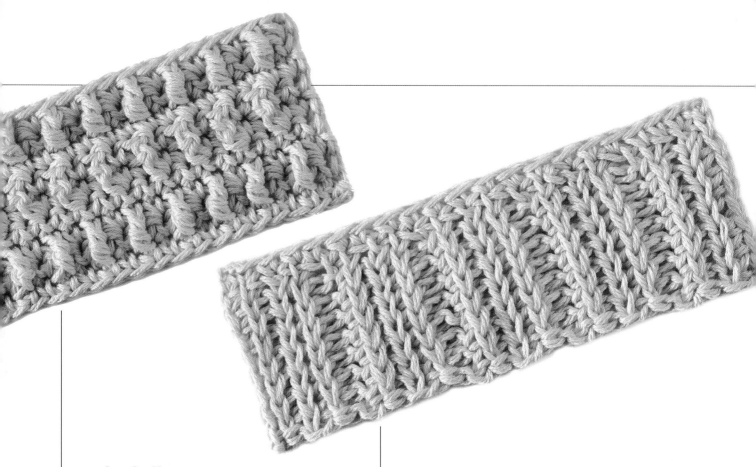

stacked rib

PATTERN NOTES

Leave stitches behind post stitches unworked.

Post stitches are worked around post of stitch 2 rows
  below throughout.

Background

Row 1 (RS): Ch an odd number of chs plus 1, sc in **back
bar** *(see illustration on page 4)* of 2nd ch from hook, and
in back bar of each ch across, turn.

Row 2: Ch 1, sc in each st across, turn.

Row 3: Ch 1, sc in first st, *****fptr** *(see Stitch Guide)*
around post of next st 2 rows below, sc in next st, rep
from * across, sc in last st, turn.

Rows 4 & 5: Rep row 2.

Row 6: Ch 1, **bptr** *(see Stitch Guide)* around post of first
st, sc in next st, [bptr around post of next st, sc in next
st] across, ending with sc in last st, turn.

Row 7: Rep row 2.

Next rows: Rep rows 2–7 consecutively to desired
length, ending with row 3 or row 6. At end of last row,
fasten off.

knitted rib

Background

Row 1 (RS): Ch any number of chs plus 1, sc in **back bar**
(see illustration on page 4) of 2nd ch from hook, and in
back bar of each ch across, turn.

Row 2: Ch 2 *(counts as first hdc)*, hdc in back bar of each
st across to last st, hdc in back bar of last st, hdc in both
lps of same st, turn.

Row 3: Ch 1, sc in back lp of each st across to last 2 sts,
sk next st, sc in last st, turn.

Row 4: Rep row 2.

Row 5: Ch 1, sc in **front bar** *(see illustration)* of each st
across, to last 2 sts, sk next st, sc in last st, turn.

Front Bar

Front Bar of Half Double Crochet

Next rows: Rep rows 2–5 consecutively to desired
length. At end of last row, fasten off.

ribs

butterfly rib

Background

Row 1 (RS): Ch 10, sc in **back bar** *(see illustration on page 4)* of 2nd ch from hook, ch 11, sk next 7 chs, sc in back bar last ch, turn.

Row 2: Ch 1, sc in first st, working in sk chs of row 1, dc in back bar of each of next 7 chs, sc in last st, turn.

Row 3: Ch 1, sc in first st, ch 9, sk next 7 dc, sc in last st, turn.

Row 4: Ch 1, sc in first st, working in sk sts, dc in each of next 7 dc, sc in last st, turn.

Rows 5 & 6: Rep rows 3 and 4.

Row 7: Ch 1, sc in first st, ch 5, sc around all ch sps below, ch 5, sk next 7 dc, sc in last st, turn.

Row 8: Rep row 4.

Row 9: Ch 1, sc in first st, ch 11, sk next 7 sts, sc in last st, turn.

Row 10: Rep row 4.

Next rows: Rep rows 3–10 consecutively to desired length, ending with row 8. At end of last row, fasten off.

back slip stitch rib

SPECIAL STITCH

Back slip stitch (back sl st): Bring yarn to front of work, insert hook as indicated from back to front so hook is facing down, yarn should be to right of hook, move yarn to left going over hook, then move yarn to right going under hook, thereby catching yarn in hook, pull yarn through st and lp on hook, turning hook counterclockwise so hook is now facing up.

Background

Row 1 (RS): Ch any number of sts, **back sl st** *(see Special Stitch)* in **back bar** *(see illustration on page 4)* of 2nd ch from hook, and in back bar of each ch across, turn.

Row 2: Ch 1, back sl st in **back lp** *(see Stitch Guide)* of each st across, turn.

Next rows: Rep row 2 to length desired. At end of last row, fasten off.

shoelace rib

PATTERN NOTES

Leave stitches behind post stitches unworked.

Post stitches are worked around post of stitches
  2 rows below.

Background

Row 1 (RS): Ch a multiple of 7 chs plus 1, sc in **back bar** (see illustration on page 4) of 2nd ch from hook, and in back bar of each ch across, turn.

Row 2: Ch 1, sc in each st across, turn.

Row 3: Ch 1, sc in first st, *yo twice, insert hook around post of st 2 rows below (mark this st), yo, pull lp through, [yo, pull through 2 lps on hook] twice, yo 4 times, sk next 3 sts 2 rows below, insert hook around post of next st, yo, pull lp through, [yo, pull through 2 lps on hook] 4 times, yo, pull through all lps on hook, sc in each of next 3 sts, yo 4 times, working in front of last post st, insert hook around post of marked st, yo, pull lp through, [yo, pull through 2 lps on hook] 4 times, yo twice, insert hook around post of st 2 rows below, yo, pull lp through, [yo, pull through 2 lps on hook] twice, yo, pull through all lps on hook**, sc in each of next 2 sts, rep from * across, ending last rep at **, sc in last st, turn.

Row 4: Rep row 2.

Row 5: Ch 1, sc in first st, ***fptr** (see Stitch Guide) around post of st 2 rows below, sc in each of next 3 sts, fptr around post of st 2 rows below**, sc in each of next 2 sts, rep from * across, ending last rep at **, sc in last st, turn.

Row 6: Rep row 2.

Row 7: Ch 1, sc in first st, *yo twice, insert hook around post of st 2 rows below (mark this st), yo, pull lp through, [yo, pull through 2 lps on hook] twice, yo 4 times, sk next 3 sts 2 rows below, insert hook around post of next st, yo, pull lp through, [yo, pull through 2 lps on hook] 4 times, yo, pull through all lps on hook, sc in each of next 3 sts, yo 4 times, working in back of last post st, insert hook around post of marked st, yo, pull lp through, [yo, pull through 2 lps on hook] 4 times, yo twice, insert hook around post of st 2 rows below, yo, pull lp through, [yo, pull through 2 lps on hook] twice, yo, pull through all lps on hook**, sc in each of next 2 sts, rep from * across, ending last rep at **, sc in last st, turn.

Rows 8 & 9: Rep rows 4 and 5.

Next rows: Rep rows 2–9 consecutively to desired length, ending with row 3 or row 6. At end of last row, fasten off.

ribs

chain stitch rib

Background

Row 1 (RS): Ch multiple of 3 chs plus 3, sc in **back bar** *(see illustration on page 4)* of 2nd ch from hook, [ch 3, sc in back bar of each of next 3 chs] across to last ch, ch 3, sc in back bar of last ch, turn.

Row 2: Sk all ch-3 sps, ch 1, sc in each st across, turn.

Row 3: Ch 1, sc in first st, [ch 3 *(push ch-3 to front of work)*, sc in each of next 3 sts] across to last st, ch 3, sc in last st, turn.

Next rows: Rep rows 2 and 3 alternately to desired length, ending with row 2. At end of last row, fasten off.

up & down

PATTERN NOTES

Leave stitches behind post stitches unworked.
Post stitches are worked around post of stitch 2 rows below throughout.

SPECIAL STITCH

Split cluster (cl): Holding back last lp of each st on hook, fptr around post of st 1 st to right, fptr around post of st 1 st to left, yo, pull through all lps on hook.

Background

Row 1 (RS): Ch multiple of 8 chs plus 2, sc in **back bar** *(see illustration on page 4)* of 2nd ch from hook, and in back bar of each ch across, turn.

Row 2: Ch 1, sc each st across, turn.

Row 3: Ch 1, sc in first st, *sk next st 2 rows below, **fptr** *(see Stitch Guide)* around post of next st, sc in next st, fptr around post of same st as last post st, sc in each of next 2 sts, **cl** *(see Special Stitch)*, sc in each of next 2 sts, rep from * across, turn.

Next rows: Rep rows 2 and 3 alternately to desired length. At end of last row, fasten off.

ladder rib

PATTERN NOTES

Leave stitches behind post stitches unworked.

Post stitches are worked around post of stitches 2 rows below throughout.

SPECIAL STITCH

Rung cluster (rung cl): Holding back last lp of each st on hook, **fpdtr** (see Stitch Guide) around post of last post st made, fptr around post st below, yo, pull through all lps on hook.

Background

Row 1 (RS): Ch multiple of 7 chs plus 1, sc in **back bar** (see illustration on page 4) of 2nd ch from hook, and in back bar of each ch across, turn.

Row 2: Ch 1, sc each st across, turn.

Row 3: Ch 1, sc in first st, ***fptr** (see Stitch Guide) around post of st 2 rows below, sc in each of next 3 sts, **rung cl** (see Special Stitch)**, sc in each of next 2 sts, rep from * across, ending last rep at **, sc in last st, turn.

Next rows: Rep rows 2 and 3 to 1 row less than desired length, ending with row 2.

Last row: Ch 1, sc in first st, *fptr around post of st 2 rows below, sc in each of next 3 sts, fptr around post of next st 2 rows below**, sc in each of next 2 sts, rep from * across, ending last rep at **, sc in last st. Fasten off.

twisted cable

PATTERN NOTES

Leave stitches behind post stitches unworked.

Post stitches are worked around post of stitch 2 rows below throughout.

Background

Row 1 (RS): Ch multiple of 7 chs plus 1, sc in **back bar** (see illustration on page 4) of 2nd ch from hook, and in back bar of each ch across, turn.

Row 2: Ch 1, sc each st across, turn.

Row 3: Ch 1, sc in first st, *sk next 3 sts 2 rows below, **fptrtr** (see Stitch Guide) around post of each of next 2 sts 2 rows below, sc in next st, working in front of last post sts, fptrtr around post of first sk st, fptrtr around post of next sk st**, sc in each of next 2 sts, rep from * across, ending last rep at **, sc in last st, turn.

Next rows: Rep rows 2 and 3 to desired length. At end of last row, fasten off.

ribs

slanted rib

PATTERN NOTES

Leave stitches behind post stitches unworked.

Post stitches are worked around post of stitches
2 rows below throughout.

Background

Row 1 (RS): Ch multiple of 7 chs plus 1,
sc in **back bar** *(see illustration on page 4)*
of 2nd ch from hook, and in back bar of each
ch across, turn.

Row 2: Ch 1, sc each st across, turn.

Row 3: Ch 1, sc in first st, *sk next 2 sts 2 rows
below, fpdtr around post of next st, sc in next
st] twice**, sc in each of next 3 sts, rep from *
across, ending last rep at **, sc in each of
last 2 sts, turn.

Next rows: Rep rows 2 and 3 alternately to
desired length. At end of last row, fasten off.

double cables

PATTERN NOTES

Leave stitches behind post stitches unworked.

Post stitches are worked around post of stitch
2 rows below throughout.

Background

Row 1 (RS): Ch multiple of 6 chs plus 2, sc in **back bar**
(see illustration on page 4) of 2nd ch from hook, and in
back bar of each ch across, turn.

Row 2: Ch 1, sc each st across, turn.

Row 3: Ch 1, sc in first st, ***fptr** *(see Stitch Guide)*
around post of each of next 2 sts 2 rows below**, sc
in next st, rep from * across, ending last rep at **, sc
in last st, turn.

Row 4: Rep row 2.

Row 5: Ch 1, sc in first st, *sk next 3 sts 2 rows below,
fptrtr *(see Stitch Guide)* around post of each of next 2
sts, sc in next st, working in front of last post sts, fptrtr
around post of first sk st, fptrtr around next sk st**, sc
in next st, rep from * across, ending last rep at **, sc in
last st, turn.

Next rows: Rep rows 2–5 consecutively to desired
length. At end of last row, fasten off.

half double crochet rib

Background

Row 1 (RS): Ch multiple of 4 chs plus 1, hdc in **back bar** *(see illustration on page 4)* of 3rd ch from hook, and in back bar of each ch across, turn.

Row 2: Ch 2 *(counts as first hdc)*, *hdc in **back lp** *(see Stitch Guide)* of each of next 2 sts**, hdc in **front lp** *(see Stitch Guide)* of each of next 2 sts, rep from * across, ending last rep at **, hdc in both lps of last st, turn.

Row 3: Ch 2, *hdc in back lp of each of next 2 sts**, hdc in front lp of each of next 2 sts, rep from * across, ending last rep at **, hdc in both lps of last st, turn.

Next rows: Rep rows 2 and 3 to desired length. At end of last row, fasten off.

zigzag rib

PATTERN NOTES

Leave stitches behind post stitches unworked.

Post stitches are worked around post of stitch 2 rows below throughout.

Background

Row 1 (RS): Ch multiple of 9 chs plus 1, sc in **back bar** *(see illustration on page 4)* of 2nd ch from hook, and in back bar of each ch across, turn.

Row 2: Ch 1, sc each st across, turn.

Row 3: Ch 1, sc in first st, *sk next 3 sts 2 rows below, **fpdtr** *(see Stitch Guide)* around post of next st, sc in each of next 2 sts, rep from * across to last 2 sts, sc in each of last 2 sts, turn.

Row 4: Rep row 2.

Row 5: Ch 1, sc in each of first 4 sts, *fpdtr around post of next st 3 sts to right**, sc in each of next 2 sts, rep from * across, ending last rep at **, sc in last st, turn.

Next rows: Rep rows 2–5 consecutively to desired length. At end of last row, fasten off.

ribs

post stitch rib

Background

Row 1 (RS): Ch any number of chs plus 2, dc in **back bar** *(see illustration on page 4)* of 4th ch from hook, and in back bar of each ch across, **do not turn**.

Row 2: Ch 2, **fpdc** *(see Stitch Guide)* around post of each st across to last st, hdc in last st, turn.

Next rows: Rep row 2 to desired length. At end of last row, fasten off.

single crochet rib

PATTERN NOTES

Change color in last stitch made. Carry color not in use up side of work.

Background

Row 1 (RS): With A, ch any number of chs plus 1, sc in **back bar** *(see illustration on page 4)* of 2nd ch from hook, and in back bar of each ch across, **changing colors** *(see Stitch Guide)* to B, turn.

Row 2: Working in **back lps** *(see Stitch Guide)*, ch 1, sc in each st across, turn.

Row 3: Working in back lps, ch 1, sc in each st across, changing to A, turn.

Row 4: Rep row 2.

Row 5: Rep row 3 changing to B.

Next rows: Rep rows 2–5 to 1 row less than desired length, ending with row 4. Fasten off B.

Last row: Rep row 2.

End row: Working in ends of rows ch 1, sc in end of each row across. Fasten off.

knit-look dishcloth

SKILL LEVEL
INTERMEDIATE

FINISHED SIZE
8 inches square

MATERIALS
- Brown Sheep Co. Cotton Fleece light (light worsted) weight yarn (3½ oz/215 yds/99g per skein):
    1 skein CW105 putty
- Size H/8/5mm crochet hook or size needed to obtain gauge

3 LIGHT

GAUGE
8 sts = 2 inches; 12 rows = 2 inches

SPECIAL STITCHES

Back slip stitch (back sl st): Bring yarn to front of work, insert hook as indicated from back to front so hook is facing down, yarn should be to right of hook, move yarn to left going over hook, then move yarn to right going under hook, thereby catching yarn in hook, pull yarn through st and lp on hook, turning hook counterclockwise so hook is now facing up.

Under back slip stitch (under back sl st): Bring yarn to front of work, insert hook as indicated from back to front so hook is facing down, yarn should be to the right of hook, move yarn to left going under hook catching yarn in hook, pull yarn through st and lp on hook, turning hook counterclockwise so hook is now facing up.

ribs

INSTRUCTIONS

BACKGROUND

Row 1 (RS): Ch 31, **back sl st** *(see Special Stitches)* in **back bar** *(see illustration on page 4)* of 2nd ch from hook, and in back bar of each ch across, turn. *(31 back sl sts)*

Row 2: Ch 1, back sl st in **back lp** *(see Stitch Guide)* is each st across, turn.

Rows 3–8: Rep row 2.

Row 9: Ch 1, back sl st in back lps of each of first 5 sts, [sl st in back lps of each of next 4 sts, **under back sl st** *(see Special Stitches)* in back lps of each of next 4 sts] twice, sl st in back lps of each of next 4 sts, back sl st in back lps of each of last 5 sts, turn.

Row 10: Ch 1, back sl st in back lps of each of first 5 sts, [under back sl st in **front lps** *(see Stitch Guide)* of each of next 4 sts, sl st in back lps of each of next 4 sts] twice, under back sl st in front lps of each of next 4 sts, back sl st in each of last 5 sts, turn.

Row 11: Ch 1, back sl st in back lp of each of first 5 sts, [sl st in back lp of each of next 4 sts, under back sl st in front lp of each of next 4 sts] twice, sl st in back lp of each of next 4 sts, back sl st in each of last 5 sts, turn.

Rows 12 & 13: Rep rows 10 and 11.

Row 14: Rep row 10.

Row 15: Ch 1, back sl st in back lps of each of first 5 sts, [under back sl st in back lp of each of next 4 sts, sl st in front lp of each of next 4 sts] twice, under back sl st in back lp of each of next 4 sts, back sl st in each of last 5 sts, turn.

Row 16: Rep row 11.

Rows 17–20: Rep rows 10 and 11 alternately.

Row 21: Ch 1, back sl st in back lp of each of first 5 sts, [sl st in front lp of each of next 4 sts, under back sl st in back lp of each of next 4 sts] twice, sl st in front lp of each of next 4 sts, back sl st in each of last 5 sts, turn.

Rows 22–33: Rep rows 10–21, ending with row 13.

Rows 34–38: Rep rows 10–14.

Row 39: Ch 1, back sl st in back lp of each of first 9 sts, [back sl st in front lps of each of next 4 sts, back sl st in back lp of each of next 4 sts] twice, back sl st in back lp of each of last 5 sts, turn.

Rows 40–46: Rep row 2.

Last row: Working around entire outer edge, [evenly sp 30 sl sts across side, ch 1 *(corner)*] 4 times, join with sl st in beg sl st. Fasten off.

beads

bunny faces

PATTERN NOTES

Using needle, thread beads onto yarn as follows; with B, thread [3 pink, 1 black, 1 pink, 1 black, 3 pink] once for every multiple of 7 sts on Background.

Change color *(see Stitch Guide)* in last stitch made.

SPECIAL STITCHES

Bead single crochet (bead sc):
When working on RS of work, insert hook as indicated, yo, pull bead up to hook, pull lp and bead through st, yo, pull through both lps on hook, bead will appear on RS of work.

When working on WS of work, pull 1 bead up to hook, sc in next st, bead will appear on RS of work.

Bunny stitch (bunny st): All of bunny is worked in 1 st and beads will appear on back of work, sl st in st indicated changing to B, ch 7, *pull bead

up to hook, sl st in back bar of 2nd ch from hook, [pull bead up to hook, sl st in back bar of next ch] twice*, [insert hook in back bar of next ch, yo, pull lp through] 3 times, **insert hook in same st as beg sl st, yo, pull lp through, [yo, pull through 2 lps on hook] twice, pull bead up to hook, yo, pull through 2 lps on hook**, ***yo, insert hook in first horizontal bar going down side of st just made, yo, pull through, insert hook in next horizontal bar going down side of st, yo, pull through***, insert hook in same st as beg sl st, yo, pull through, yo, pull through 2 lps on hook, pull bead up to hook, [yo, pull through 2 lps on hook] twice, rep between *** once, rep between ** once, yo, pull through all lps on hook, ch 1 to close, ch 4, rep between * once, sk closing ch, sl st in first horizontal bar going

down side of bunny face, [sl st in next horizontal bar going down side of bunny face] twice, sl st in same st as beg sl st, changing to A.

Background

Row 1: With A, ch multiple of 7 chs plus 1, sc in **back bar** *(see illustration on page 4)* of 2nd ch from hook, and in back bar of each ch across, turn.

Row 2: Ch 1, sc in each st across, turn.

Row 3 (WS): Ch 1, sc in each of first 2 sts, *sl st in next st, **bunny st** *(see Special Stitches)* in next st, sl st in next st**, sc in each of next 4 sts, rep from * across, ending last rep at **, sc in each of last 2 sts, turn.

Row 4 (RS): Ch 1, sc in each of first 2 sts, *sc in next sl st, ch 1, sk next bunny st, sc in next sl st**, sc in each of next 4 sts, rep from * across, ending last rep at **, sc in each of last 2 sts, turn.

beads

Row 5: Ch 1, sc in each st and each ch across, turn.

Row 6: Rep row 2.

Row 7: Ch 1, sc in each of first 2 sts, ◊*insert hook in next st, insert hook through any lp at base of bunny's ear, yo, pull lp through ear and st, yo, pull through 2 lps on hook*, sc in next st, rep between * once◊◊, sc in each of next 4 sts, rep from ◊ across, ending last rep at ◊◊, sc in each of last 2 sts, turn.

Rows 8 & 9: Rep row 2. At end of last row, fasten off.

Tie

Make 1 for each Bunny.

With any color, cut 1 strand of yarn 10 inches long for each bunny. Attach center of strand to row 2 under bunny st, ties ends in bow. Trim ends to desired length.

surface chains

SPECIAL STITCHES

Surface stitch (surface st): Holding yarn at back of work, insert hook in sp between sts, yo, pull lp through sp and lp on hook.

Surface bead stitch (bead st): Holding yarn at back of work, insert hook in sp between sts, yo, pull up 2 beads to hook, pull lp and both beads through sp and lp on hook, there are now 2 beads on the lp which is on the hook, arrange the beads so there is 1 bead on each side of hook.

Background

Row 1: Ch 4, sc in **back bar** *(see illustration on page 4)* of 2nd ch from hook, and in back bar of each ch across, turn.

Row 2: Ch 1, sc in each st across, turn.

Next rows: Rep row 2 to desired length working a multiple of 4 rows plus 3. At end of last row, fasten off.

Beads

Using needle, thread 16 beads onto yarn for every multiple of 4 rows on Background, then thread 8 more beads.

Using **surface st** *(see Special Stitches)* and **bead st** *(see Special Stitches)*, work according to chart.

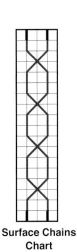

Surface Chains Chart

STITCH KEY
- ▪ Surface st
- ▫ Bead st

loop fringe

PATTERN NOTE

Using needle, thread 7 beads onto yarn for every multiple
of 2 stitches on edging.

Background

Row 1: Ch 1, *pull up 7 beads to hook, ch 2, rep from *
until all beads have been used, ch 1.

Row 2 (RS): Sc in 2nd ch from hook, *sc inside next
lp of beads, sc between 2 lps of beads, rep from * across
to last lp of beads, sc inside next lp of beads, sc in last
ch, turn.

Row 3: Ch 1, sc in each st across, turn.

Next rows: Work in desired pattern. At end of last row,
fasten off.

knotted loops

PATTERN NOTE

Using needle, thread 12 beads onto yarn for every
multiple of 2 stitches on Background.

Background

Row 1: Ch multiple of 2 chs plus 2, sc in **back bar** *(see
illustration on page 4)* of 2nd ch from hook, and in back
bar of each ch across, turn.

Row 2: Ch 1, sc in first st, *pull 12 beads up to hook,
leaving 2½-inch sp between the 6th and 7th bead, hdc in
next st, sc in next st, rep from * across. Fasten off.

Knots

With yarn in sp between 6th and 7th beads, tie knot at
the bottom of each bead lp as shown in photo.

beads

ocean pearls

PATTERN NOTE

Using needle, thread 7 beads onto yarn for every multiple of 6 stitches on Background.

SPECIAL STITCH

Bead double crochet (bead dc): Yo, insert hook as indicated, yo, pull lp through, yo, pull through 2 lps on hook, pull up bead, yo, pull through 2 lps on hook, bead will appear on back side of work.

Background

Row 1: Ch multiple of 6 chs plus 2, sc in **back bar** *(see illustration on page 4)* of 2nd ch from hook, and in back bar of each ch across, turn.
Row 2: Ch 1, insert hook in first st, yo, pull lp through, pull up bead to st, yo, pull through 2 lps on hook, *sk next 2 sts, 5 **bead dc** *(see Special Stitch)* in next st, pull up bead to hook, sk next 2 sts**, insert hook in next st, yo, pull lp through, pull up bead to st, yo, pull through 2 ps on hook, rep from * across, ending last rep at **, sc in last st. Fasten off.

tri-chain fringe

PATTERN NOTE

Using needle, thread 12 beads onto yarn.

Background

Row 1: Ch odd number of chs plus 1, sc in **back bar** *(see illustration on page 4)* of 2nd ch from hook, and in back bar of each ch across, turn.
Row 2: Ch 1, sc in each st across, turn.

Fringe

Sl st in first st.
First strand: Ch 1, [ch 1, pull 2 beads through ch, tighten ch so the beads do not go back through, place 1 bead on each side of hook, pull another bead up to last ch, yo, pull yarn only through lp on hook] 4 times, ch 1. Fasten off.

Next strand: Thread 12 beads onto yarn, sk next st, join with sl st in next st, rep first strand.
Rep next strand across.

chain fringe

PATTERN NOTE

Using needle, thread 9 beads onto yarn for every multiple of 2 stitches on Background plus another 9 beads.

Background

Row 1 (RS): Ch multiple of 2 chs plus 2, sc in **back bar** *(see illustration on page 4)* of 2nd ch from hook, and in back bar of each ch across, turn.

Row 2: Sl st in first st, *[pull up 1 bead to hook, ch 1] 9 times, working back across beads and ch just made, sl st in first ch with bead, sl st in each of next 8 chs with beads**, sl st in each of next 2 sts on Background, rep from * across, ending last rep at **, sl st in last st on Background. Fasten off.

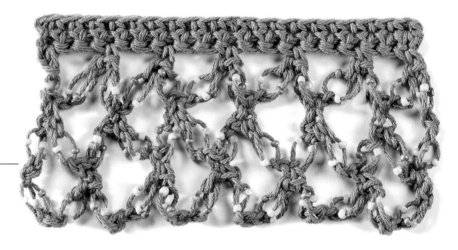

triple love knots

PATTERN NOTE

Using needle, thread 18 beads onto yarn for every multiple of 3 stitches on Background plus another 6 beads.

SPECIAL STITCHES

Beginning tri-bead love knot (beg love knot): Ch 1, pull 2 beads through ch, tighten ch so beads do not go back through, place 1 bead on each side of hook, pull lp on hook up 1 inch, pull another bead up to last ch, yo, pull yarn only through lp, sc in back strand of lp at top of lp just above the last bead which was pushed forward.

Beaded love knot (beaded love knot): Work beg love knot twice.

Background

Row 1: Ch multiple of 3 chs plus 2, sc in **back bar** *(see illustration on page 4)* of 2nd ch from hook, and in back bar of each ch across, turn.

Row 2: Ch 1, sc in each st across, turn.

Row 3: Ch 1, sc in first st, [**beaded love knot** *(see Special Stitches)*, sk next 2 sts, sc in next st] across, turn.

Row 4: Ch 1, sc in first st, **beg love knot** *(see Special Stitches)*, beaded love knot, sc in center sc of first beaded love knot, [beaded love knot, sc in center sc of next beaded love knot] across, turn.

Row 5: Rep row 4. Fasten off.

beads

beaded rib

PATTERN NOTE

Using needle, thread 7 beads onto yarn for every multiple of 2 rows of desired length.

Background

Row 1: Ch 8, yo, pull 1 bead up to hook, pull lp and bead through lp on hook, *bead is now on lp which is on the hook, fix bead so it is on right-hand side of hook, bead will appear on **back lp** *(see Stitch Guide)* of next st*, insert hook in **back bar** *(see illustration on page 4)* of 2nd ch from hook, **yo, pull lp through, yo, pull 1 bead up to hook, pull lp and bead through both lps on hook, rep between * once, insert hook in back bar of next ch, rep from ** across to last ch, sc in back bar of last ch, turn. *(7 sc)*

Row 2: Ch 1, sc in **back lp** *(see Stitch Guide)* of each st across, turn.

Row 3: Yo, pull 1 bead up to hook, pull lp and bead through lp on hook, *bead is now on the lp which is on the hook, fix bead so that it is on the right-hand side of hook*, **insert hook in back lp of next st, yo, pull lp through, yo, pull 1 bead up to hook, pull lp and bead through both lps on hook, rep between * once, rep from ** across to last st, sc in back lp of last st, turn.

Next rows: Rep rows 2 and 3 alternately to desired length, ending with row 2.

Last row: Ch 1, sc in end of each row across. Fasten off.

lark's head

PATTERN NOTE

Thread 21 beads onto yarn for every multiple of 2 stitches on Background.

Background

Row 1 (RS): Ch multiple of 2 chs plus 2, sc in **back bar** *(see illustration on page 4)* of 2nd ch from hook, and in back bar of each ch across, turn.

Row 2: Sl st in each of first 2 sts, *pull up 3-inch lp on hook, pull 21 beads through lp, remove lp from hook, pull lp tight to completely close, insert hook in next st, yo, pull through**, sl st in next st, rep from * across, ending last rep at **. Fasten off.

picot points

PATTERN NOTE

Thread 5 beads onto yarn for every multiple of 5
   stitches on Background.

Background

Row 1 (RS): Ch multiple of 5 chs plus 3, sc in **back
bar** *(see illustration on page 4)* of 2nd ch from hook,
and in back bar of each ch across, turn.

Row 2: Ch 1, sc in each of first 2 sts, *ch 2, [pull
bead up to hook, ch 1] 4 times, pull 1 bead to hook,
sl st in 4th ch from hook, ch 3, sk next 3 sts, sc in
each of next 2 sts, rep from * across. Fasten off.

ruffled loops

PATTERN NOTE

Using needle, thread 5 beads onto yarn for every
   multiple of 2 stitches on Background.

Background

Row 1 (WS): Ch multiple of 2 chs plus 2, sc in **back
bar** *(see illustration on page 4)* of 2nd ch from hook,
[pull up 5 beads to hook, hdc in back bar of next ch, sc
in back bar of next ch] across, turn.

Row 2: Ch 1, sc in each of first 2 sts, [hdc in next st, sc
in next st] across to last st, sc in last st, turn.

Row 3: Ch 1, sc in first st, [pull up 5 beads to hook, hdc
in next st, sc in next st] across, turn.

Rows 4 & 5: Rep rows 2 and 3. At end of last row,
fasten off.

beads

up & down fringe

PATTERN NOTE

Thread 14 beads onto yarn for every multiple of 4 stitches on Background.

Background

Row 1 (WS): Ch multiple of 4 chs plus 2, sc in **back bar** *(see illustration on page 4)* of 2nd ch from hook, and in back bar of each ch across, turn.

Row 2: Ch 1, sc in each st across, turn.

Row 3: Sl st in first st, *[pull 1 bead up to hook, ch 1] 7 times, pull 1 bead up to hook, sk next st, sl st in next st, [pull 1 bead up to hook, ch 1] 5 times, pull 1 bead up to hook, sk next st, sl st in next st, rep from * across. Fasten off.

vertical rib

PATTERN NOTE

Thread 5 beads of 1 color, then 5 beads of another color onto yarn for every multiple of 2 stitches on Background.

Background

Row 1 (RS): Ch multiple of 2 chs plus 2, sc in **back bar** *(see illustration on page 4)* of 2nd ch from hook, and in back bar of each ch across, turn.

Row 2: Ch 1, sc in first st, [pull 10 beads up to hook, leaving a small sp between the 5th and 6th bead, ch 1, sk next st, sc in next st] across, turn.

Row 3: Ch 1, sc in each st and ch across, turn.

Row 4: Ch 1, sc in each st across, turn.

Row 5: Ch 1, sc in first st, [sc in bead lp between 5th and 6th bead, sk next st on this row, sc in next st] across. Fasten off.

twisted loops

PATTERN NOTE

Using needle, thread 12 beads onto yarn for every multiple of 2 stitches on Background.

Background

Row 1 (RS): Ch multiple of 2 chs plus 4, sc in **back bar** *(see illustration on page 4)* of 2nd ch from hook, and in back bar of each ch across, turn.

Row 2: Ch 1, sc in each of first 2 sts, [pull 12 beads up to hook, leaving a little slack between 6th and 7th beads, hdc in next st, sc in next st] across to last st, sc in last st, turn.

Row 3: Ch 4 *(counts as first dc and ch-1)*, [inserting hook from back of lp to front of lp in sp left between 6th and 7th beads, sl st in bead lp, ch 1] across, to last st, dc in last st, turn.

Row 4: Ch 1, sc in first st, [sc in next ch-1 sp, sc in bead lp] across ending with sc in next ch-1 sp, sc in last st. Fasten off.

trinity fringe

PATTERN NOTE

Using needle, thread 17 beads onto yarn for every multiple of 5 stitches on Background.

Background

Row 1 (RS): Ch multiple of 5 chs plus 1, sc in **back bar** *(see illustration on page 4)* of 2nd ch from hook, and in back bar of each ch across, turn.

Row 2: Sl st in each of first 3 sts, *ch 1, pull 5 beads up to hook, ch 1, pull 7 beads up to hook, ch 1, pull 5 beads up to hook, ch 1, sl st in same st as last sl st**, sl st in each of next 5 sts, rep from * around, ending last rep at **, sl st in each of last 2 sts. Fasten off.

beads

beaded wrap

FINISHED SIZES

Instructions given fit woman's small/
medium; changes for large/X-large
are in [ ].

FINISHED GARMENT MEASUREMENTS

Bust: 43½ inches *(small/medium)* [48½
inches *(large/(X-large)*]

MATERIALS

- Brown Sheep Co. Cotton
  Fleece light (light worsted)
  weight yarn (3½ oz/215 yds/
  99g per skein):
     4 skeins CW560 my blue heaven
- Sizes G/6/4mm and H/8/5mm crochet
  hooks or size needed to obtain gauge
- Tapestry needle
- Opaque rainbow seed beads: 1,148
  [1,242]
- 1-inch pin back

GAUGE

Size H hook: 7 sts = 2¼ inches; 13 rows =
4 inches
Take time to check gauge.

SPECIAL STITCHES

Surface stitch (surface st):
Holding yarn at back of work, insert hook in sp between sts, yo, pull lp through sp and lp on hook.

Surface bead stitch (surface bead st): Holding yarn at back of work, insert hook in sp between sts, yo, pull 2 beads up to hook, pull lp and both beads through sp and lp on hook, there are now 2 beads on the lp which is on the hook, arrange the beads so there is 1 bead on each side of hook.

Bead single crochet (bead sc):
Pull 1 bead up to hook, sc in next st, bead will appear on RS of work.

INSTRUCTIONS

WRAP

Row 1: With size H hook, ch 49, sc in **back bar** *(see illustration on page 4)* of 2nd ch from hook, sc in back bar of each ch across, turn. *(48 sc)*

Rows 2–4: Ch 1, sc in each st across, turn.

Row 5: Ch 1, sc in both lps of each of first 4 sts, [sc in **front lp** *(see Stitch Guide)* of next st, sc in **back lp** *(see Stitch Guide)* of next st] across to last 4 sts, sc in both lps of last 4 sts, turn.

Rows 6-136 [6-152]: Rep row 5.

Rows 137-140 [153-156]: Rep row 2.

Yoke

Row 1: Working in end of rows, ch 2 *(counts as first hdc)*, hdc in end of each of next 2 [1] rows, ***hdc dec** *(see Stitch Guide)* in end of next 2 rows, hdc in end of each of next 5 [4] rows, rep from * 18 [24] times, hdc dec in end of next 2 rows, hdc in end of each of last 2 rows, turn. *(120 [130] sts)*

Row 2: Ch 2, [**fpdc** *(see Stitch Guide)* around next st, **bpdc** *(see Stitch Guide)* around next st] across to last st, hdc in last st, turn.

Rows 3–6: Rep row 2.

Trim

Working around outer edge of entire Wrap, with size H hook, ch 1, evenly sp sc down side, around bottom and back up next side, working 3 sc in corners, to opposite side. Fasten off.

beads

Surface Stitches

With beading needle, thread 920 [984] beads onto yarn. The 4 sc rows at beg of the Wrap and the 4 sc rows at the end of the Wrap form the sides of the Wrap, the 4 sc at the ends of the rows on the Wrap on the opposite end from the Yoke form the bottom of the Wrap; work **surface st** and **surface bead st** *(see Special Stitches)* on sides and bottom of Wrap according to chart.

Beaded Fringe

*Cut 1 strand of yarn 7 inches long, tie knot in end of yarn as close to end as possible then thread 5 beads onto yarn. With needle, sew the other end of yarn randomly spaced below edge of Yoke in 4 sts on the ends of the rows on the Wrap, rep *42 [48] times or as desired.

PIN

Rnd 1 (WS): With beading needle, thread 18 beads onto yarn, leaving long end at beg, form ring with yarn,

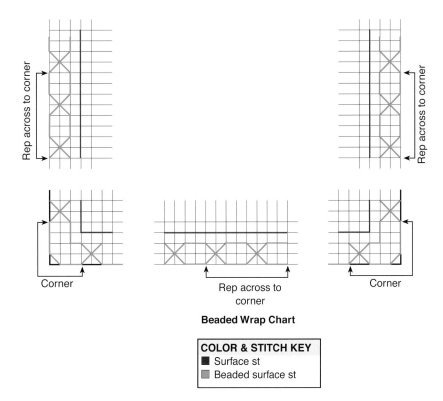

Rep across to corner

Corner

Rep across to corner

Rep across to corner

Corner

Rep across to corner

Beaded Wrap Chart

COLOR & STITCH KEY
■ Surface st
▪ Beaded surface st

with size G hook, ch 1, **bead sc** *(see Special Stitches)* 6 times in ring, pull end to tighten, do not join. *(6 bead sc)*

Rnd 2 (WS): 2 bead sc in back lp of each st around. *(12 bead sc)*

Rnd 3: [Sl st in next st, ch 1] around, join with sl st in beg sl st. Fasten off. With long end, sew pin back to WS of Pin.

Attach Pin to front opening to close Wrap.

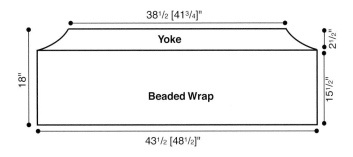

38½ [41¾]"

Yoke

2½"

18"

15½"

Beaded Wrap

43½ [48½]"

sculpture

anchors away!

SPECIAL STITCH

Surface stitch (surface st):
Holding yarn at back of work, insert hook between sts, yo, pull lp through st and lp on hook.

Background

Row 1: Ch 12, sc in **back bar** *(see illustration on page 4)* of 2nd ch from hook, and in back bar of each ch across, turn.

Row 2: Ch 1, sc in each st across, turn.

Next rows: Rep row 2 to desired length working a multiple of 7 rows. At end of last row, fasten off.

Ropes

Work **surface st** *(see Special Stitch)* on Background as shown on chart.

Life Ring

Make 1 for every 7 rows on Background.

Ch 18, sl st in first ch to form ring, sl st in **back lp** *(see Stitch Guide)* of each ch around, join with sl st in beg sl st, back of sts is RS of work. Fasten off.

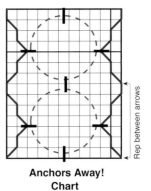

**Anchors Away!
Chart**

STITCH KEY
☐ Background
■ Surface st
■ Lifesaver placement
▣ Long st

Assembly

1. Place Life Rings RS up, evenly sp across Background between Ropes.

2. Using tapestry needle and long st, sew Life Ring to Background and Ropes according to chart.

pretty bows in a row

Background

Row 1: Ch multiple of 9 chs plus 1, sc in **back bar** *(see illustration on page 4)* of 2nd ch from hook, and in back bar of each ch across, turn.

Row 2: Ch 1, sc in each st across, turn.

Rows 3 & 4: Rep row 2.

Row 5: Ch 1, sc in each of first 4 sts, *ch 21, sl st in back bar of 2nd ch from hook and in back bar of each ch across, sc in each of next 2 sts, ch 21, sl st in back bar of 2nd ch from hook and in back bar of each ch across**, sc in each of next 7 sts, rep from * across, ending last rep at **, sc in each of last 3 sts, turn.

Row 6: Ch 1, keeping strands in back of work, sc in each st across, turn.

Rows 7–8: Rep row 2. At end of last row, fasten off. Tie strands into bows.

sculpture

granny squares

SPECIAL STITCH

Surface stitch (surface st): Holding yarn at back of work, insert hook between sts, yo, pull lp through st and lp on hook.

Background

Row 1: Ch multiple of 8 chs plus 1, sc in **back bar** *(see illustration on page 4)* of 2nd ch from hook, and in back bar of each ch across, turn.

Row 2: Ch 1, sc in each st across, turn.

Rows 3–9: Rep row 2. At end of last row, fasten off. Work **surface sts** *(see Special Stitch)* on Background, beg with largest square and ending with smallest square as shown on chart.

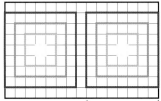

Rep between arrows
**Granny Squares
Chart**

COLOR & STITCH KEY
☐ Background
■ Surface st B
▨ Surface st C
▨ Surface st D
☐ Surface st E

basket weave

Background

Row 1: With A, ch 11, sc in **back bar** *(see illustration on page 4)* of 2nd ch from hook [ch 2, sk next 2 chs, sc in back bar of next ch] across, turn.

Row 2: Ch 1, sc in first st, [ch 2, sk next ch-2 sp, sc in next st] across, turn.

Next rows: Rep row 2 to 1 row less than desired length, last row will be WS of work. Drop lp from hook, do not fasten off.

First Weaving Strip

Row 1: With WS facing, join B with a sc in back bar of sk ch on starting ch of row 1, sc in back bar of next sk ch, turn.

Row 2: Ch, sc in each st across, turn.

Next rows: Rep row 2 until there are the same number of rows as Background. At end of last row, fasten off.

Center & Last Weaving Strip

Row 1: With WS facing, join B with a sc in back bar of next sk ch on starting ch on opposite side of row 1 on Background, sc in next sk ch, turn.

Next rows: Rep row 2 and next rows of First Weaving Strip.

Weaving

Weave Strips in and out of ch-2 sp as desired or as follows:

First and Last Strips: Sk first sp, weave up through next sp, [sk next 2 sps, weave down through next sp, up through next sp] across until all sps are used.

Center Strip: Weave up through first sp, sk next sp, [down through next sp, up through next sp, sk next 2 sps] across until all sps are used.

Background Continued

Next row: Pick up dropped lp of A, ch 1, sc in first st, [sc in each of next 2 sts on Strip, sk next ch-2 sp on Background, sc in next st on Background] across, **do not turn**.

Last row: Working in ends of rows, ch 1, evenly sp sc across ends of rows. Fasten off.

twisted

Background

Row 1 (RS): With A, ch 6, sc in **back bar** *(see illustration on page 4)* of 2nd ch from hook, and in back bar of each ch across, turn.

Row 2: Ch 1, sc in first st, [ch 1, sk next st, sc in next st] across, turn.

Row 3: Ch 1, sc in each st and in each ch across, turn.

Rows 4–7: Ch 1, sc in each st across, turn.

Next rows: Rep rows 2–7 consecutively to 1 row less than desired length, ending with row 7. Do not fasten off, drop lp from hook.

First Side Rope

Row 1: With RS facing, join B with sc to first sk st on the right-hand side on row 1 of Background, turn.

Row 2: Ch 1, sc in st, turn.

Rows 3–6: Rep row 2.

Row 7: Ch 1, insert hook in st then insert hook in sk st on Background 6 rows directly above, yo, pull lp through sk st and st, yo, pull through all lps on hook, turn.

Next rows: Rep rows 2–7 consecutively until all sk sts going up Background have been used, then rep rows 2–6 once. At end of last row, fasten off.

2nd Side Rope

Note: Wind C into ball small enough to go under First Side of Rope before beg.

Row 1: With RS facing, join C with sc in 2nd sk st on row 1 of Background, turn.

Row 2: Ch 1, sc in st, turn.

Rows 3–6: Rep row 2.

Row 7: Drop lp from hook, push ball of yarn and 2nd Side of Rope from left to right under First Side of Rope then take 2nd Side of Rope from right to left over First Side of Rope, pick up dropped C lp, ch 1, insert hook in st then insert hook in sk st on Background 6 rows directly above, yo, pull lp through sk st and st, yo, pull through all lps on hook, turn.

Next rows: Rep rows 2–7 consecutively until all sk sts going up Background have been used, then rep rows 2–6 once. At end of last row, fasten off.

Background Continued

Last row: With WS facing, put 2nd Side of Rope from left to right under First Side of Rope then put 2nd Side of Rope from right to left over First Side of Rope, pick up dropped lp of A on Background, ch 1, sc in first st, working through both thicknesses sc in last st on 2nd Side of Rope and next st on Background at same time, sc in next st on Background only, sc in last st on First Side of Rope and Background at same time, sc in last st on Background only. Fasten off.

sculpture

open braid

PATTERN NOTES

Post stitches are worked around post of
  stitches 2 rows below throughout.
Leave stitches behind post stitches unworked.

Background

Row 1: Ch 8, sc in **back bar** *(see illustration on page 4)* of 2nd ch from hook, and in back bar of each ch across, turn.

Row 2: Ch 1, sc in each st across, turn.

Row 3: Ch 1, sc in first st, **fptr** *(see Stitch Guide)* around next st, sc in next st, sk next 2 sts 2 rows below, **fpdtr** *(see Stitch Guide)* around next st, sc in next st, working in front of last post st, fpdtr around first sk st, sc in last st, turn.

Row 4: Rep row 2.

Row 5: Ch 1, sc in first st, sk next 2 sts 2 rows below, fpdtr around next st, sc in next st, working in back of last post st, fpdtr around first sk st, sc in next st, fptr around next st, sc in last st, turn.

Next rows: Rep rows 2–5 consecutively to desired length, ending with row 3 or row 5. At end of last row, fasten off.

tumbling pass

PATTERN NOTE

Wind yarn into 2 separate balls
  before beginning.

Background

Row 1: Ch multiple of 4 chs plus 3, sc in **back bar** *(see illustration on page 4)* of 2nd ch from hook, and in back bar of each ch across, turn.

Row 2: Ch 1, sc in each of first 2 sts, [ch 2, sk next 2 sts, sc in each of next 2 sts] across, turn.

Rows 3: Ch 1, sc in each st and in each ch across, turn.

Rows 4–7: Ch 1, sc in each st across, turn.

Row 8: Ch 1, sc in each st across, turn. Do not fasten off. Drop lp from hook.

First Flip

Row 1: With RS facing, join 2nd ball of yarn with sc in first sk st on row 1 of Background, sc in next sk st, turn.

Row 2: Ch 1, sc in each st across, turn.

Rows 3–7: Rep row 2. At end of last row, fasten off.

Remaining Flips

Row 1: With RS facing, join 2nd ball of yarn with sc in next sk st on row 1 of Background, sc in next sk st, turn.

Rows 2–7: Rep rows 2–7 of First Flip.

Background Continued

Last row: Pick up dropped lp, ch 1, sc in each of first 2 sts, [twist Flip directly below 1 half turn clockwise, working through both thicknesses of Background and Flip at same time, sc in each of next 2 sts, sc in each of next 2 sts on Background only] across. Fasten off.

springing stitches

SPECIAL STITCH

Spring stitch (spring st): Yo 7 times, insert hook as indicated, yo, pull lp through, yo, pull through 8 lps on hook, yo, pull through last 2 lps on hook.

Background

Row 1: Ch odd number of chs plus 1, sc in **back bar** *(see illustration on page 4)* of 2nd ch from hook, [ch 1, sk next ch, sc in back bar of next ch] across, turn.
Row 2: Ch 3 *(counts as first dc)*, [**spring st** *(see Special Stitch)* in next ch sp, dc in next st] across, turn.
Row 3: Ch 1, sc in first st, [ch 1, sk next spring st, sc in next st] across, turn. Fasten off.

hollow coils

Background

Row 1: With A, ch any number of chs plus 1, sc in **back bar** *(see illustration on page 4)* of 2nd ch from hook, and in back bar of each ch across, turn.
Row 2: Ch 1, sc in each st across, turn.
Rows 3–7: Rep row 2. At end of last row, fasten off.

Hollow Coil

Rnd 1: With B, ch 4, sl st in first ch to form ring, ch 1, 5 sc in ring, do not join.
Rnd 2: Sc in **back lp** *(see Stitch Guide)* of each st around.
Next rnds: Rep rnd 2 until Hollow Coil is approximately 2⅓ times longer than Background.
Test size of Coil by placing coil on Background, twisting coil every 2 inches, top of Coil should be on row 6 and bottom of Coil should be on row 2, Coil should stretch from 1 end of Background to other end of Background. If Coil is the correct size, sew ends tog, if Coil is not the correct size, add more rnds or unravel rnds as needed for perfect fit, then sew coil ends tog.
Sew Hollow Coil to Background.

sculpture

loop de loop

Background

Row 1: Ch 8, sc in **back bar** *(see illustration on page 4)* of 2nd ch from hook, sc in back bar of next ch, ch 6, sc in back bar of each of last 3 chs, turn.

Row 2: Ch 1, keeping chain lps in back of work, sc in each st across, turn.

Row 3: Ch 1, sc in each of first 2 sts, ch 12, sc in each of next 3 sts, ch 12, sc in each of last 2 sts, turn.

Row 4: Rep row 2.

Row 5: Ch 1, sc in each of first 2 sts, ch 8, sc in each of next 3 sts, ch 8, sc in each of last 2 sts, turn.

Next rows: Rep rows 2–5 consecutively to desired length. At end of last row, fasten off.

Weaving

Number the lps in the first column in number order beg with the first ch-6 lp as number 1a, the ch-12 lp above it as 2a, the ch-8 lp above that as 3a, until they are all numbered. Then, number the lps in the 2nd column in the same manner, numbering them as 1b, 2b, 3b, etc.

1. Lift number 1a lp up, insert number 2a lp through 1a lp from the back;

2. Pull 2a lp up, lift 1b lp up insert 2b lp through 1b lp from the back, pull 2b lp up;

3. Insert 3a lp through 2b lp from back, lift 3a lp up;

4. Insert 3b lp through 2a lp from back, lift 3b lp up;

5. Insert 4a lp through 3a lp from back, lift 4a lp up;

6. Insert 4b lp through 3b lp from back, lift 4b lp up;

Continue in like fashion until all lps are woven.

Last row: Ch 1, sc in first st, [working in 1 ch lp and in next st at same time, sc in each of next 2 sts] across. Fasten off.

zigzag rickrack

Background

Row 1: With A, ch any number of chs plus 1, sc in **back bar** *(see illustration see page 4)* of 2nd ch from hook, and in back bar of each ch across, turn.

Row 2: Ch 1, sc in each st across, turn.

Rows 3–6: Rep row 2. At end of last row, fasten off.

Rickrack

Rnd 1: With B, ch 4, sc in first ch, turn.

Row 2: Ch 4, sc in sc, turn.

Next rows: Rep row 2 until Rickrack is same length as Background. At end of last row, fasten off.

With tapestry needle, sew Rickrack to 3rd row on Background.

chevron weave

PATTERN NOTES

Post stitches are worked around post of stitches 2 rows
   below throughout.

Leave stitches behind post stitches unworked.

Change color in last stitch made.

Carry yarn not being used on wrong side of work.

SPECIAL STITCH

Closing single crochet (closing sc): Insert hook in
back lp *(see Stitch Guide)* of sk st 2 rows below then
insert hook in st 1 row below this row, yo, pull lp
through st and back lp, yo, pull through both lps on hook.

Background

Row 1: With A, ch 9, sc in **back bar** *(see illustration on
page 4)* of 2nd ch from hook, and in back bar of each ch
across, turn.

Row 2: Ch 1, sc in each st across, turn.

Row 3: Ch 1, sk first st 2 rows below, *fptr *(see Stitch
Guide)* around next st, **changing color** *(see Stitch Guide)*
to B, working in front of last post st, fptr around sk st
changing to A**, sk next st, rep from * across,
ending last rep at **, turn.

Row 4: Ch 1, **closing sc** *(see Special Stitch)* in each
st across, changing to B in last st, turn.

Row 5: Ch 1, **fpdc** *(see Stitch Guide)* around first st,
changing to A, [sk next st 2 rows below, fptr around next
st, changing to B working in back of last post st, fptr in sk
st, changing to A] 3 times, fpdc around last st, turn.

Row 6: Ch 1, close sc in each st across, turn.

Next rows: Rep rows 3–6 consecutively to desired length,
ending with row 4 or row 6. At end of last row, fasten off.

woven spike stitch

PATTERN NOTES

When working spike stitch, if strands
   of yarn in spike stitch twist when
   spike stitch is make, untwist them
   before proceeding.

Background

Row 1: Ch 8, sc in **back bar** *(see
illustration on page 4)* of 2nd ch from
hook, and in back bar of each ch
across, turn.

Row 2: Ch 1, sc in each st
across, turn.

Rows 3 & 4: Rep row 2.

Row 5: Ch 1, sc in first st, insert
hook in st 4 rows below and 4 sts
to left, *yo, pull lp through and up
even with this row, yo, pull through
all lps on hook*, sc in each of next 3
sts, working in front of last spike st,
insert hook in st 4 rows below and 4
sts to right, rep between * once, sc
in last st, turn.

Row 6: Rep row 2.

Row 7: Ch 1, sc in first st, working
in front of spike st 2 rows below,
insert hook in st 4 rows below and
4 sts to left, *yo, pull lp through
and up even with this row, yo, pull
through all lps on hook*, sc in each
of next 3 sts, working in front of
last spike st and in back of spike st
2 rows below, insert hook in st

4 rows below and 4 sts to right, rep
between * once, sc in last st, turn.

Next rows: Rep rows 6 and 7 alternately to desired length, ending with
row 7. At end of last row, fasten off.

sculpture

diamonds & bobbles

PATTERN NOTES

Post stitches are worked around post of stitches 2 rows below throughout.

Leave stitches behind post stitches unworked.

SPECIAL STITCHES

Closing single crochet (closing sc): Insert hook in **back lp** *(see Stitch Guide)* of sk st 2 rows below then insert hook in st 1 row below this row, yo, pull lp through st and back lp, yo, pull through both lps on hook.

Front post bobble (fp bobble): Yo, insert hook around post of st 2 rows below, yo, pull lp through and up even with this row, [yo, insert hook around post of same st, yo, pull lp through and up even with this row] twice, yo, pull through all lps on hook.

Background

Row 1: Ch 10, sc in **back bar** *(see illustration on page 4)* of 2nd ch from hook, and in back bar of each ch across, turn.

Row 2: Ch 1, sc in each st across, turn.

Row 3: Ch 1, sc in each of first 4 sts, **fptr** *(see Stitch Guide)* around next st 2 rows below, sc in each of last 4 sts, turn.

Row 4: Ch 1, sc in each sc and **closing sc** *(see Special Stitches)* in each post st across, turn.

Row 5: Ch 1, sc in each of first 2 sts, sk next 2 sts 2 rows below, fptr around next st, sc in each of next 3 sts, fptr around post of same st as last post st, sc in each of last 2 sts, turn.

Row 6: Rep row 4.

Row 7: Ch 1, sk first 2 sts 2 rows below, fptr around next st, sc in each of next 3 sts, **fp bobble** *(see Special Stitches)*, sc in each of next 3 sts, yo twice, insert hook around post of st 2 sts to right, yo, pull lp through, [yo, pull through 2 lps on hook] twice, insert hook in last st on this row, yo, pull lp through st and all lps on hook, turn.

Row 8: Rep row 4.

Row 9: Ch 1, sc in each of first 2 sts, fptr around post of st 2 sts to right, sc in each of next 3 sts, sk next 2 sts 2 rows below, fptr around next st, sc in each of last 2 sts, turn.

Row 10: Rep row 4.

Row 11: Ch 1, sc in each of first 4 sts, yo twice, insert hook around post of st, 2 sts to right, *yo, pull lp through, [yo, pull through 2 lps on hook] twice*, yo, sk next st 2 rows below, insert hook around post of next st, yo, pull lp through, yo, pull through 2 lps on hook, yo twice, sk next st 2 rows below, insert hook around post of next st, rep between * once, yo, pull through all lps on hook, sc in each of last 4 sc, turn.

Row 12: Rep row 4.

Next rows: Rep rows 3–12 to desired length. At end of last row, fasten off.

garden lattice

SPECIAL STITCH

Surface stitch (surface st): Holding yarn at back of work, insert hook between sts, yo, pull lp through st and lp on hook.

Background

Row 1: With A ch any number of chs plus 1, sc in **back bar** *(see illustration on page 4)* of 2nd ch from hook, and in back bar of each ch across, turn.

Rows 2–11: Ch 1, sc in each st across, turn. At end of last row, fasten off.

With B, work **surface st** *(see Special Stitch)* on Background as shown on chart.

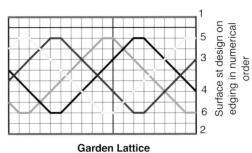

Surface st design on edging in numerical order

Garden Lattice Chart

COLOR KEY
- ☐ Background
- ■ Surface sts No. 1 & No. 2
- ■ Surface st No. 3
- ■ Surface st No. 4
- ☐ Surface st No. 5
- ▨ Surface st No. 6

x marks the spot

PATTERN NOTES

Post stitches are worked around post of stitches 2 rows below throughout. Leave stitches behind post stitches unworked.

Background

Row 1: Ch 10, sc in **back bar** *(see illustration on page 4)* of 2nd ch from hook, and in back bar of each ch across, turn.

Row 2: Ch 1, sc in each st across, turn.

Row 3: Ch 1, sc in first st, [sk next 2 sts 2 rows below, **fpdtr** *(see Stitch Guide)* around next st, sc in next st, working in front of last post st, fpdtr around first sk st, sc in next st] across, turn.

Row 4: Rep row 2.

Row 5: Ch 1, sc in first st, **fptr** *(see Stitch Guide)* around next st, sc in next st, sk next 2 sts 2 rows below, fpdtr around next st, sc in next st, working in back of last post st, fpdtr around first sk st, sc in next st, fptr around next st, sc in last st, turn.

Next rows: Rep rows 2–5 consecutively, ending with row 3 or row 5. At end of last row, fasten off.

sculpture

spike stitch afghan

SKILL LEVEL

■■■
EXPERIENCED

FINISHED SIZE

47 x 54 inches

MATERIALS

- Brown Sheep Cotton Fleece light (light worsted) weight yarn (3½ oz/ 215 yds/99g per skein):

  16 skeins #CW230 Victorian pink

- Size H/8/5mm crochet hook or size needed to obtain gauge

GAUGE

27 sts = 8 inches; 32 rows = 8 inches

PATTERN NOTES

When working spike stitch, if strands of yarn in spike stitch twist when stitch is made, untwist them before proceeding.

Use Special Stitches to work Patterns.

SPECIAL STITCHES

Spike stitch (spike st): Insert hook as indicated, yo, pull lp through and up even with this row, yo, pull through all lps on hook.

Spike stitch A (spike st A): Spike st in st 4 rows below and 4 sts to left, placing hook in front of spike st 2 rows below.

Spike stitch B (spike st B): Spike st in st 4 rows below and 4 sts to right, placing hook in front of last spike st and in back of spike st 2 rows below.

Double spike stitch (double spike st): First part: insert hook in first indicated st, *yo, pull lp through and up even with this row*, yo, pull through 1 lp on hook; **2nd part:** insert hook in next indicted st, rep between * once, yo, pull through all lps on hook.

Double spike stitch A (double spike A): Work first part of double spike st in st 4 rows below and 4 sts to right placing

hook in front of first spike st in path and in back of next spike st in path to indicated st.

Double spike stitch B (double spike B): Work 2nd part of double spike st in st 2 rows below and 2 sts to left.

Double spike stitch C (double spike C): Work first part of double spike st in st 2 rows below and 2 sts to right.

Double spike stitch D (double spike D): Work 2nd part of double spike st in st 4 rows below and 4 sts to left, placing hook in front of spike st 2 rows below.

Double spike stitch E (double spike E): Work 2nd part of double spike st in st 4 rows below and 4 sts to left.

Double spike stitch F (double spike F): Work first part of double spike st in st 2 rows below and 2 sts to right placing hook in back of last spike st worked.

Double spike stitch G (double spike G): Work first part of double spike st in st 4 rows below and 4 sts to right, placing hook in back of first spike st in path *(last spike st worked)*, in front of next spike st in path and in back of last spike st in path to indicated st.

Double spike stitch H (double spike H): Work 2nd part of double spike st in st 2 rows below and 2 sts to left, placing hook in front of spike st 2 rows below.

Double spike stitch I (double spike I): Work 2nd part of double spike st in st 4 rows below and 4 sts to left, placing hook in back of spike st 2 rows below.

Triple spike stitch (triple spike st): Insert hook in st 3 rows below and 2 sts to right, *yo, pull lp through and up even with this row*, insert hook in st 3 rows below, rep between * once, insert hook in st 3 rows below and 2 sts to left, rep between * once, yo, pull through all lps on hook.

Spike cross-stitch (spike cross-st): Sk next 2 sts 3 rows below, spike st in next st 3 rows below, sc in next st on this row, working

sculpture

in front of last spike st, spike st in first sk st 3 rows, below.

PATTERNS

Woven Spike Stitch

Work over 159 sts using Special Stitches as needed.

Row 1 (WS): Ch 1, sc in each st across, turn.

Row 2 (RS): Ch 1, sc in first st, spike st A, [sc in each of next 3 sts, double spike A, double spike B, sc in each of next 33 sts, double spike E, double spike D] 4 times, sc in each of next 3 sts, spike st B, sc in last st, turn.

Row 3: Rep row 1.

Row 4: Ch 1, sc in first st, spike st A, *sc in each of next 3 sts, double spike A, double spike E, sc in next st, double spike F, double spike E, sc in next st, [double spike G, double spike E, sc in next st] 13 times, double spike G, double spike D, sc in next st, double spike G, double spike H, sc in next st, double spike G, double spike D, rep from * 3 times, sc in each of next 3 sts, spike st B, sc in last st, turn.

Row 5: Rep row 1.

Column

Work over 7 sts using Special Stitches as needed.

Row 1 (RS): Sc in first st, spike st A, sc in each of next 3 sts, spike st B, sc in next st.

Row 2: Sc in each of next 7 sts.

Rows 3–36: Rep rows 1 and 2 alternately.

Row 37: Rep row 1.

Triple Spike

Work over 31 sts using Special Stitches as needed.

Row 1 (RS): Sc in each of next 31 sts.

Row 2: Rep row 1.

Row 3: [Sc in each of next 3 sts, triple spike st, sc in each of next 2 sts] 5 times, sc in next st.

Row 4: Sc in each of next 3 sts, *[**bpsc** (see Stitch Guide) around the 6 strands of the triple spike st*, sc in each of next 5 sts] 4 times, rep between *, sc in each of next 3 sts.

Row 5: Rep row 1.

Row 6: Rep row 1.

Row 7: Sc in each of next 6 sts, [triple spike st, sc in each of next 5 sts] 4 times, sc in next st.

Row 8: Sc in each of next 6 sts, [bpsc around the 6 strands of the triple spike st, sc in each of next 5 sts] 4 times, sc in next st.

Rows 9–32: Rep rows 1–8 consecutively.

Rows 33–37: Rep rows 1–5.

Spike Cross

Work over 31 sts using Special Stitches as needed.

Row 1 (RS): Sc in each of next 31 sts.

Row 2: Rep row 1.

Row 3: [Spike cross-st, sc in next st] 7 times, spike cross-st.

Row 4: Rep row 1.

Row 5: Sc in each of next 2 sts, [spike cross-st, sc in next st] 7 times, sc in next st.

Rows 6–33: Rep rows 2–5 consecutively.

Rows 34–36: Rep rows 2–4.

Row 37: Rep row 1.

Spike

Work over 31 sts using Special Stitches as needed.

Row 1 (RS): Sc in each of next 31 sts.

Row 2: Rep row 1.

Row 3: [Spike st in st 3 rows below, sc in next st] 15 times, spike st in st 3 rows below.

Row 4: Rep row 1.

Row 5: [Sc in next st, spike st in next st 3 rows below] 15 times, sc in next st.

Rows 6–33: Rep rows 2–5 consecutively.

Rows 34–36: Rep rows 2–4.

Row 37: Rep row 1.

INSTRUCTIONS

AFGHAN

Note: Use Special Stitches as needed.

Row 1 (RS): Ch 160, sc in **back bar** (see illustration on page 4) of 2nd ch from hook and in back bar of each ch across, turn.

Row 2: Ch 1, sc in each st across, turn.

sculpture

Row 3: Ch 1, sc in first st, *spike st in st 2 rows below and 2 sts to left*, [sc in each of next 3 sts, rep between * once, sc in each of next 33 sts, **spike st in next st 2 rows below and 2 sts to right **] 4 times, sc in each of next 3 sts, rep between ** once, sc in last st, turn.

Row 4: Rep row 2.

Row 5: Ch 1, sc in first st, spike st in st 4 rows below and 4 sts to left, *sc in each of next 3 sts, double spike A, double spike E, sc in next st, [double spike G, double spike E, sc in next st] 14 times, double spike G, double spike D, sc in next st, double spike G, double spike I, sc in next st**, double spike G, double spike E, rep from * across, ending last rep at **, double spike G, double spike D, sc in each of next 3 sts, spike st in st 4 rows below and 4 sts to right working in front of first spike st in path and in back of last spike st in path to indicated st, sc in last st, turn.

Row 6: Rep row 2.

Row 7: Ch 1, work first row of each of the following Patterns: Column, Triple Spike, Column, Spike Cross, Column, Spike, Column, Triple Spike, Column, turn.

Row 8: Ch 1, work next row of each of the following Patterns: Column, Triple Spike, Column, Spike, Column, Spike Cross, Column, Triple Spike, Column, turn.

Row 9: Ch 1, work next row of the following Patterns: Column, Triple Spike, Column, Spike Cross, Column, Spike, Column, Triple Spike, Column, turn.

Rows 10–43: [Rep rows 8 and 9 alternately] 17 times, continuing to work subsequent rows of each Pattern.

Rows 44–48: Work Woven Spike Stitch Pattern.

Row 49: Ch 1, work first row of the following Patterns: Column, Spike Cross, Column, Spike, Column, Triple Spike, Column, Spike Cross, Column, turn.

Row 50: Ch 1, work next row of the following Patterns: Column, Spike Cross, Column, Triple Spike, Column, Spike, Column, Spike Cross, Column, turn.

Row 51: Ch 1, work the next row of the following Patterns: Column, Spike Cross, Column, Spike, Column, Triple Spike, Column, Spike Cross, Column, turn.

Rows 52–85: [Rep rows 50 and 51 alternately] 17 times, continuing to work subsequent rows of each pattern.

Rows 86–90: Work Woven Spike Stitch Pattern.

Row 91: Ch 1, work first row of the following Patterns: Column, Spike, Column, Triple Spike, Column, Spike Cross, Column, Spike, Column, turn.

Row 92: Ch 1, work next row of the following Patterns: Column, Spike, Column, Spike Cross, Column, Triple Spike, Column, Spike, Column, turn.

Row 93: Ch 1, work next row of the following Patterns: Column, Spike, Column, Triple Spike, Column, Spike Cross, Column, Spike, Column, turn.

Rows 94–127: [Rep rows 92 and 93 alternately] 17 times, continuing to work subsequent rows of each pattern.

Rows 128–132: Work Woven Spike Stitch Pattern.

Rows 133–211: Rep rows 7–85.

Rows 212–214: Work Woven Spike Stitch Pattern, rows 1–3.

Row 215: Ch 1, sc in first st, spike st A, sc in next st, double spike F, double spike I, sc in next st, *double spike G, double spike E, sc in next st, double spike F, double spike E, sc in next st, [double spike G, double spike E, sc in next st] 14 times, double spike G, double spike B, sc in next st, double spike G, double spike D, sc in next st**, double spike G, double spike I, sc in next st, rep from * across ending last rep at **, double spike G, double spike B, sc in next st, spike st in st 4 rows below and 4 sts to right placing hook in back of first spike st in path, in front of next spike st in path and in back of last spike st in path to indicated st, sc in last st, turn.

Row 216: Rep row 2.

Rnd 217: Now working around entire Afghan in sts and in ends of rows, evenly sp sl st around with ch 1 at each corner, join with sl st in beg sl st. Fasten off.

fringe

CHAPTER SIX

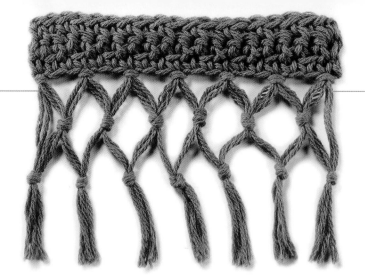

knotted fringe

Top

Row 1 (RS): Ch multiple of 3 chs plus 2, sc in **back bar** *(see illustration on page 4)* of 2nd ch from hook, and in back bar of each ch across, turn.

Next rows: Work any pattern as desired. At end of last row, fasten off.

Fringe

Cut strands of yarn twice as long as desired fringe length, plus 3 inches

for all knots. Cut 2 strands of yarn for first st on row then cut 2 strands of yarn for every 3rd st.

Fold 2 strands of yarn in half with WS of work facing, insert hook in st where Fringe is to be attached, pull fold through st, pull ends through fold. Pull ends to tighten. Fringe in every 3rd st along bottom edge of Background.

First Knots

Take half the strands of 1 Fringe and half of the strands from the Fringe

next to it and tie them tog *(see Illustration)* 1 inch from the top. Rep across.

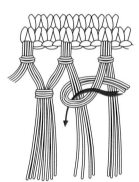

Knotted Fringe

2nd Knots

Take the unknotted strands from the first Fringe and half the stands from the next fringe and tie them tog 1 inch below the last knot. Continue across Fringe.

---

sideways chains

PATTERN NOTES

Leave stitches behind post stitches unworked throughout. Post stitches are worked around post of stitches 2 rows below.

Background

Row 1 (RS): Ch 15, sl st in **back bar** *(see illustration on page 4)* of 2nd ch from hook, sl st in back bar in each of next 8 chs, sc in back bar of last 5 chs, turn.

Row 2: Ch 1, sc in each of first 5 sts, ch 10, leaving rem sts unworked, turn.

Row 3: Sl st in back bar of 2nd ch from hook and in back bar of each of next 8 chs, sc in next st, [**fptr** *(see Stitch Guide)* around next st, sc in next st] twice, turn.

Row 4: Rep row 2.

Row 5: Sl st in back bar of 2nd ch from hook, sl st in back bar of each of next 8 chs, sc in next st, sk next 2 sts 2 rows below, fpdtr around next st, sc in next st, working in front of last post st, fpdtr around first sk st, sc in last st, turn.

Next rows: Rep rows 2–5 consecutively to desired length ending with row 3 or row 5. At end of last row, fasten off.

fringe

faux beads

Top

Row 1: Ch multiple of 6 chs plus 1, sc in **back bar** *(see illustration on page 4)* of 2nd ch from hook, and in back bar of each ch across, turn.

Row 2: Ch 1, sc in first st, [sc in **front lp** *(see Stitch Guide)* of next st, sc in **back lp** *(see Stitch Guide)* of next st] across to last st, sc in both lps of last st, turn.

Row 3: Rep row 2. Fasten off.

Fringe

Cut 1 strand yarn 15 inches long for every 3 sts on Background.

Fold strand in half, pull fold through st, pull ends through fold. Pull ends to tighten.

Beg in 2nd st from end, Fringe in every 3rd st across.

Beads

Make 3 beads of various colors for each Fringe.

Round

Rnd 1: Ch 2, 6 sc in 2nd ch from hook, **do not join**. *(6 sc)*

Rnd 2: 2 sc in each st around, join with sl st in beg sc. Leaving long end, fasten off.

Weave long end through sts on last rnd, stuff with a little piece of same color yarn, pull tight to close. Secure end.

Flat

Rnd 1: Ch 2, 8 sc in 2nd ch from hook, **do not join**. Pull end to tighten. *(8 sc)*

Rnd 2: Sl st in each st around, join with sl st in beg sl st. Fasten off.

Assembly

Tie knot in first Fringe ½ inch from top, *with tapestry needle, thread bead onto Fringe, slip bead up to knot, tie another knot just below bead, [tie knot ½ inch from below last knot, thread bead on Fringe, tie knot just below bead] twice, rep from * across all Fringe.

Trim ends of Fringe as desired.

dangling balls

Ball

Make 1 Ball for every multiple of 4 sts on Background.

Rnd 1: Ch 2, 4 sc in 2nd ch from hook, **do not join**. *(4 sc)*

Rnd 2: 2 sc in each st around. *(8 sc)*

Rnd 3: Sc in each st around.

Rnd 4: Rep rnd 3. Leaving long end, fasten off.

Stuff Ball with small amount of fiberfill. Weave long end through sts on last rnd, pull to close. Secure end.

Top

Row 1: Ch multiple of 4 chs plus 21, sc in **back bar**

(see illustration on page 4) of 2nd ch from hook, and in back bar of each ch across, turn.

Row 2: Ch 1, sc in each st across, turn.

Row 3: Ch 1, sc in first st, [ch 4, sl st in top of Ball, ch 4, sk next 3 sts on Background, sc in next st] across. Fasten off.

traditional fringe

Top

Row 1 (RS): Ch any number of chs, plus 1, sc in **back bar** *(see illustration on page 4)* of 2nd ch from hook, and in back bar of each ch across, turn.

Next rows: Work in any pattern as desired.

Fringe

Cut strands of yarn twice as long as desired Fringe length plus 1 inch to allow knot. Cut 1 strand for each st across bottom of Background.

Fold strand in half, pull fold through st, pull ends through fold. Pull to tighten.

Fringe in each st across bottom of Background.

slip stitch fringe

PATTERN NOTES

Cut yarn in desired length.

Hold 4 strands of Fringe yarn together throughout.

Use 1 strand of yarn to work slip stitches.

Fringe

Row 1 (RS): [Fold 4 strands in half, sl st in fold around center of all strands, ch 1] across until all Fringe has been used.

Row 2: With RS facing and holding yarn at back of work, sl st around first 8 strands, [sl st around next 4 strands] across to last 8 strands, sl st around all 8 strands.

Row 3: With RS facing, ch 1, sl st around first 8 strands, [sl st around next 4 strands] across to last 8 strands, sl st around last 8 strands, join with sl st in turning ch-1 of last row. Fasten off.

double bullions

Background

Row 1 (WS): Ch any number of chs plus 1, sc in **back bar** *(see illustration on page 4)* of 2nd ch from hook, and in back bar of each ch across, turn.

Row 2: Ch 1, sc in **front lp** *(see Stitch Guide)* of first st, *pull up 4½-inch lp on hook, turn hook clockwise 15 times, sl st in top of last st**, sc in front lp of next st, rep from * across, ending last rep at **, sc in front lp of last st, turn.

Row 3: Working in **back lps** *(see Stitch Guide)* of sts on row 1, sc in each st across, turn.

Row 4: Ch 1, sc in first st, *pull up 4½-inch lp on hook, turn hook clockwise 15 times, sl st in top of last st**, sc in front lp of next st, rep from * across, ending last rep at **, sc in last st. Fasten off.

fringe

interlocking rings

Ring Set

Make 1 set for every 5 sts on Background.

Note: *Rings within Ring set can be made in alternating colors if desired.*

First Ring

Ch 14, sl st in **back bar** *(see illustration on page 4)* of first ch to form ring, sl st in back bar of each ch around, join with sl st in beg sl st. Fasten off.

2nd Ring

Ch 14, insert ch through center of last Ring, sl st in back bar of first ch to form ring, sl st in back bar of each ch around, join with sl st in beg sl st. Fasten off.

3rd Ring

Rep 2nd Ring.

Top

Row 1: Ch multiple of 5 chs plus 2, sc in back bar of 2nd ch from hook, and in back bar of each ch across, turn.

Row 2: Ch 1, sc in each st across, turn.

Row 3: Ch 1, sc in each of first 3 sts, *ch 1, with RS of Ring facing, insert hook inside First Ring from front to back, yo, pull lp through Ring and lp on hook, drop lp from hook, insert hook in dropped lp from back side of Ring, sl st in back ridge of ch**, sc in each of next 5 sts, rep from * across, ending last rep at **, sc in each of last 3 sts. Fasten off.

braided pigtails

Top

Row 1: With A, ch 16, sc in **back bar** *(see illustration on page 4)* of 2nd ch from hook, and in back bar of each ch across, turn. Fasten off.

Row 2: Join B with sc in first st, sc in each of next 2 sts, ch 13, leaving rem sts unworked, turn.

Row 3: Sc in back bar of 2nd ch from hook and back bar of each ch across, sc in each of last 3 sts, turn. Fasten off.

Row 4: With C, rep row 2.

Row 5: Rep row 3.

Row 6: With A, rep row 2.

Row 7: Rep row 3.

Next rows: Rep rows 2–7 consecutively to desired length ending with row 4.

Next row: Rep row 3. Do not fasten off.

Last row: Working in ends of rows, **changing colors** *(see Stitch Guide)* in last st made, matching colors, sc in end of each row across. Fasten off.

Braid

Cut 1 strand of yarn 10 inches long. Braid first 3 colors on Top tog, tie strand around braids in double knot. Trim ends of bow desired.

Rep across.

dressed-up dolls

PATTERN NOTE
Requires 3½ inch and 4-inch pieces of cardboard.

Top
Row 1: Ch multiple of 9 chs plus 1, sc in **back bar** *(see illustration on page 4)* of 2nd ch from hook, and in back bar of each ch across, turn.

Row 2: Ch 1, sc in each st across. Fasten off.

Doll
Make 1 for every multiple of 9 sts on Top
Body
Wrap yarn around 4-inch piece of cardboard 30 times for Body.

For **hanger**, cut strand of yarn 10 inches long, slide Body off cardboard, insert strand through 1 end of Body lps and tie securely leaving long ends. Cut lps open at other end.

Head
Cut another strand of yarn 6 inches long, wrap around Body ¾ inch from top.

Arms
Wrap yarn around 3½ inch piece of cardboard 10 times. Slide Arms off cardboard.

Divide Body in half for front and back, slide Arms between the 2 layers. Cut 10-inch strand of yarn and tie around Body just below Arms to form waist.

Trim Body length to 3 inches. Cut ends of lps on Arms. Trim Arms to 2½ inches across.

Cut 2 strands each 6 inches long. Tie 6-inch strands around ends of Arms for hands.

Poncho
Make 1 for each Doll.
Row 1: Ch 2, sc in back bar of 2nd ch from hook, turn.

Row 2: Ch 1, sc in st, turn.

Rows 3–5: Rep row 2.

Row 6: Ch 1, sc in st, do not turn.

Row 7: Ch 1, sc in left side of last sc, turn.

Rows 8–12: Rep row 2. At end of last row, fasten off. Sew end of row 1 to end of row 12.

Fringe
Cut 2½-inch strand of yarn for each Fringe. Fold strand in half, pull fold through, pull ends through fold. Pull to tighten.

Evenly sp Fringe around bottom edge of Poncho.

Place 1 Poncho on each Doll.

Sk first 4 sts, attach Doll to next st, [sk next 8 sts, attach Doll] across Top until all Dolls are used.

fringe

popped popcorn

PATTERN NOTES

Post stitches are worked around post of
   stitches 2 rows below throughout.
Leave stitches behind post stitches
   unworked.

SPECIAL STITCH

Popcorn (pc): Holding back last lp of each st on hook,
3 dc in next st, yo, pull through all lps on hook.

Background

Row 1: Ch 14, sc in **back bar** *(see illustration on page 4)*
of 2nd ch from hook, and in back bar of each ch across, turn.

Row 2: Ch 1, sc in each of first 5 sts, **pc** *(see Special
Stitch)* in next st, sc in each of next 5 sts, ch 1, sk next st,
sc in last st, turn.

Row 3: Ch 1, sc in first st, sc in ch-1 sp, sc in each of
next 8 sts, **fptr** *(see Stitch Guide)* around each of next 2
sts, sc in last st, turn.

Row 4: Ch 1, sc in each of first 4 sts, ch 10, leaving rem
sts unworked, turn.

Row 5: Sc in back bar of 2nd ch from hook, and in back
bar of each of next 8 chs, sc in next st, fptr around each
of next post sts, sc in last st, turn.

Next rows: Rep rows 2–5 consecutively to desired
length, ending with row 3. Fasten off.

Push popcorn through each ch-1 sp on Background to
button it.

tied up in knots

PATTERN NOTES

Wind yarn into 5 separate balls or use
   5 separate skeins.
Hold 4 strands together for loops.

Background

Row 1: Holding 4 strands tog *(fringe
yarn)* and free ends of fringe yarn to the
right with bulk of fringe yarn to the left,
using single strand of yarn, sl st around
all 4 strands 3 inches from end, *move
bulk of fringe yarn from left to right
crossing over single strand and leaving
6-inch lp of fringe yarn to the left, sl
st around fringe yarn**, move bulk of
fringe yarn from right to left crossing
over single strand of yarn, do not leave
a lp on right side, sl st around fringe
yarn, rep from * till desired length,
ending last rep at ** and working a
multiple of 6 sl sts, turn clockwise so
lps are to the right. Leaving 3-inch end,
fasten off fringe yarn.

Row 2: Ch 1, [with single strand, sl st
around 4 stands of fringe yarn in 6-inch
lp, sl st around 4 strands of fringe yarn to
outside of 6-inch lp] across, turn counterclockwise so the lps are to the left.

Row 3: Ch 1, [with single strand,
sl st around 4 strands of fringe yarn
in 6 inch lp, sl st around 4 strands of
fringe yarn to outside of 6-inch lp]
across. Fasten off.

Holding first 3 lps of fringe yarn
(24 strands) tog, tie 1 large knot in
center of all strands. Rep across using
set of 3 lps for each knot.

hairpin fringe

PATTERN NOTES

Take top crossbar off hairpin lace loom. Set prongs 2½ inches apart.

Background

Row 1: Make a slip knot in yarn and place on left prong, replace top crossbar, take yarn from left to right across front of loom, then from right to left across back of loom. Insert hook in slip knot *(keep slip knot as small as possible, but at the same time large enough to be able to insert hook to make sts)*, yo, pull through sl st, ch 1 *(there should be a very small lp toward left prong and a very large lp toward right prong)*, sc in front strand of small lp toward left prong.

Row 2: Drop lp from hook, insert hook into dropped lp from the back of the loom, turn loom clockwise once so the large lp is now to the left and the small lp is to the right, yo, pull through lp on hook, sc in front strand of large lp which is to the left.

Row 3: Drop lp from hook, insert hook in dropped lp from the back of the loom, turn loom clockwise once so small lp is now to the left and large lp is to the right, yo, pull through lp on hook, sc in front strand of small lp which is to the left.

Next rows: Rep rows 2 and 3 alternately to desired length, ending with row 3.

Last row: Take top crossbar off loom. Slide Background off prongs, turn so small lps are at the top, ch 1, [insert hook in small lp from back to front, yo, pull lp through, yo, pull through all lps on hook] across. Fasten off.

Cut end of each large lp open.

curly qs

Background

Row 1 (RS): Ch 4, sc in **back bar** *(see illustration on page 4)* of 2nd ch from hook, and in back bar of each ch across, turn.

Row 2: Ch 1, sc in each st across, turn.

Row 3: Ch 1, sc in each st across, ch 18, turn.

Row 4: 2 dc in back bar of 4th ch from hook, 3 dc in back bar of each of next 13 chs, (dc, hdc, sc) in back bar of last ch, sc in each of last 3 sts, turn.

Row 5: Rep row 2.

Next rows: Rep rows 2–5 consecutively to desired length, ending with row 2. At end of last row, fasten off.

fringe

yo-yos

Yo-yo

Make 1 for every 6 sts on Background.

Rnd 1 (RS): Ch 4, 11 dc in 4th ch from hook *(first 3 chs count as first dc)*, join with sl st in top of beg ch-3. *(12 dc)*

Rnd 2: Ch 3 *(counts as first dc)*, dc in each st around, join with sl st in 3rd ch of beg ch-3. Leaving long end, fasten off. Turn WS out.

Weave long end through sts on rnd 2, pull to close. Secure end.

Top

Row 1 (RS): Ch multiple of 6 chs plus 1, sc in **back bar** *(see illustration on page 4)* of 2nd ch from hook, and in back bar of each ch across, turn.

Row 2: Ch 1, sc in first st, [sc in **front lp** *(see Stitch Guide)* of next st, sc in **back lp** *(see Stitch Guide)* of next st] across to last st, sc in both lps of last st, turn.

Row 3: Ch 1, sc in each of first 3 sts, *drop lp from hook, with WS of Yo-yo facing, insert hook from left to right through st at top of Yo-yo, pick up dropped lp and pull through st on Yo-yo**, sc in each of next 6 sts, rep from * across, ending last rep at **, sc in each of last 3 sts. Fasten off.

perfect pompoms

PATTERN NOTE

Requires 2-inch piece of cardboard.

Pompom

Make 1 for every 6 sts on Top.

Wrap yarn around cardboard 50 times, carefully slide lps off cardboard. Cut 1 strand of yarn 10 inches long, tie strand around center of lps, cut lps, trim as desired.

Top

Row 1 (RS): Ch multiple of 6 chs plus 5, sc in **back bar** *(see illustration on page 4)* of 2nd ch from hook, and in back bar of each ch across, turn.

Row 2: Ch 1, sc in first st, [sc in **front lp** *(see Stitch Guide)* of next st, sc in **back lp** *(see Stitch Guide)* of next st] across to last st, sc in both lps of last st, turn.

Row 3: Ch 1, sc in each of first 2 sts, *ch 5, sl st in back bar of 2nd ch from hook and in back bar of each ch across**, sc in each of next 3 sts, ch 7, sl st in Pompom, sl st in back bar of 2nd ch from hook and in back bar of each ch across, sc in each of next 3 sts, rep from * across, ending last rep at **, sc in each of last 2 sts. Fasten off.

banded tassels

PATTERN NOTES

Post stitches are worked around post of stitches 2 rows below throughout.

Leave stitches behind post stitches unworked.

Design requires 3-inch piece of cardboard.

SPECIAL STITCH

Front post treble crochet cluster (fptr cl): Holding back last lp of each st on hook, fptr around post of st 1 st to right, fptr around post of st 1 st to left, yo pull through all lps on hook.

Top

Row 1 (RS): Ch multiple of 9 chs plus 1, sc in **back bar** (see illustration on page 4) of 2nd ch from hook, and in back bar of each ch across, turn.

Row 2: Ch 1, sc in each st across, turn.

Row 3: Ch 1, sc in first st, *[fptr cl (see Special Stitch), sc in next st] 4 times, sc in next st, rep from * across, turn.

Row 4: Rep row 2.

Row 5: Ch 1, sc in each of first 2 sts, *[fptr cl, sc in next st] 3 times**, sc in each of next 3 sts, rep from *

across, ending last rep at **, sc in last st, turn.

Row 6: Rep row 2.

Row 7: Ch 1, sc in each of first 3 sts, *[fptr cl, sc in next st] twice**, sc in each of next 5 sts, rep from * across, ending last rep at **, sc in each of last 2 sts, turn.

Row 8: Rep row 2.

Row 9: Ch 1, sc in each of first 4 sts, * fptr cl**, sc in each of next 8 sts, rep from * across, ending last rep at **, sc in each of last 4 sts. Fasten off.

Tassel

Make 1 for every multiple of 9 sts on Background.

Wrap yarn around 3-inch cardboard 50 times.

For **hanger**, cut strand 10 inches in length, insert strand under lps at 1 end of cardboard and tie tightly around all lps. Slide lps off cardboard. Cut lps at other end.

Tie 8-inch strand around all strands ¾-inch below first strand.

Band

Make 1 for each Tassel.

Ch 8, sl st in back bar of first ch to form ring, sl st in back bar of each ch around, join with sl st in beg sl st. Fasten off.

Pull hanger of Tassel and top of Tassel through Band so Band is covering 8-inch strand.

Trim ends as desired.

With hanger, attach each Tassel to each cl on last row of Background.

fringe

cut loops

PATTERN NOTE

Design requires 2½ inch piece of cardboard.

SPECIAL STITCH

Loop single crochet (lp sc): Wrap yarn from front to back around cardboard, sc in next st, this will create a lp in back of work, remove lp from cardboard.

Background

Row 1 (WS): Ch any number of chs plus 1, **lp sc** *(see Special Stitch)* in 2nd ch from hook and in each ch across, turn.

Row 2: Ch 1, sc in each st across, turn. Fasten off.

Cut end of each lp open, or lps can be left uncut if desired.

love knots

Top

Row 1: Ch multiple of 2 chs plus 1, sc in **back bar** *(see illustration on page 4)* of 2nd ch from hook, and in back bar of each ch across, turn.

Row 2: Ch 1, sc in first st, [sc in **front lp** *(see Stitch Guide)* of next st, sc in **back lp** *(see Stitch Guide)* of next st] across to last st, sc in last st, turn.

Row 3: Ch 1, sc in first st, *[pull up 1-inch lp, yo, pull lp through lp, sc in back strand of lp] 3 times, pull up 1-inch lp, yo, pull lp through lp, insert hook in back strand of lp, yo, pull through, insert hook in top of last sc, yo, pull through st and all lps on hook**, sc in each of next 2 sts, rep from * across, ending last rep at **, sc in last st. Fasten off.

dangling chains

Top

Row 1 (RS): Ch multiple of 2 chs plus 1, sc in **back bar** *(see illustration on page 4)* of 2nd ch from hook, and in back bar of each ch across, turn.

Row 2: Ch 1, sc in first st, [sc in **front lp** *(see Stitch Guide)* of next st, sc in **back lp** *(see Stitch Guide)* of next st] across to last st, sc in both lps of last st, turn.

Row 3: Ch 1, sc in first st, [ch 10, sl st in back bar of 2nd ch from hook and in back bar of each ch across, sc in next st] across. Fasten off.

elegant candelabras

PATTERN NOTES

Post stitches are worked around
post of stitches 2 rows below
throughout.

Leave stitches behind post
stitches unworked.

Background

Row 1: Ch multiple of 10 chs plus 2,
sc in **back bar** *(see illustration on
page 4)* of 2nd ch from hook, and in
back bar of each ch across, turn.

Row 2: Ch 1, sc in each st
across, turn.

Row 3: Ch 1, sc in each of first 3 sts,
*[sk next 2 sts 2 rows below, **fpdtr**
(see Stitch Guide) around next st,
sc in next st, **fptr** *(see Stitch Guide)*
around same st as last post st, sc in
next st, fpdtr around same st as last
post st**, sc in each of next 5 sts,
rep from * across, ending last rep at
**, sc in each of last 3 sts, turn.

Row 4: Rep row 2.

Row 5: Ch 1, sc in first st *[sk next
2 sts 2 rows below, fpdtr around
next post st, sc in next st] twice, fptr
around same st as last post st, sc in
next st, fpdtr around same st as last
post st, sc in next st, fpdtr around
post st 3 sts to right, sc in next st,
rep from * across, turn.

Row 6: Rep row 2.

Row 7: Ch 1, sc in first st, [fptr
around next st, sc in next st]
across, turn.

Row 8: Rep row 2. Fasten off.

Fringe

Cut 5 strands, each 10 inches in
length. Fold strands in half, pull
fold through st, pull ends through
fold. Pull to tighten.

Attach Fringe in bottom of each
st where 3 post sts group has
been work across bottom edge
of Background.

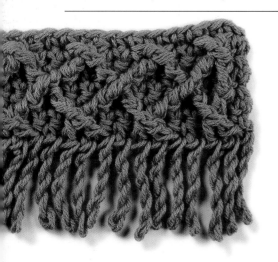

bordered bullions

PATTERN NOTES

Leave stitches behind post stitches
unworked throughout.

Post stitches are worked around post
of stitches 2 rows below.

Background

Row 1 (RS): Ch multiple of 4 chs plus
2, sc in **back bar** *(see illustration on
page 4)* of 2nd ch from hook, and in
back bar of each ch across, turn.

Row 2: Ch 1, sc in each st
across, turn.

Row 3: Ch 1, sc in first st, [sk
next 2 sts 2 rows below, **fpdtr** *(see
Stitch Guide)* around next st, sc in
next st, work in front of last post st,
fpdtr around first sk st, sc in next st]
across, turn.

Row 4: Rep row 2.

Row 5: Ch 1, sc in first st, **fptr** *(see
Stitch Guide)* around next st, sc in
next st, [sk next 2 sts 2 rows below,
fpdtr around next st, sc in next st,
working in back of last post st, fpdtr
around first sk st, sc in next st]
across to last 2 sts, fptr around next
st, sc in last st, turn.

Row 6: Rep row 2.

Row 7: Ch 1, sc in first st, *pull
up 4½-inch lp on hook, turn hook
clockwise 10 times, sl st in top of
last sc, sk next 2 sts 2 rows below,
fpdtr around next st, pull up 4½-inch
lp on hook, turn hook clockwise 10
times, sl st in top of last st, sc in
next st, pull up 4½-inch lp on hook,
turn hook clockwise 10 times, sl st
in top of last sc, working in front
of last post st, fpdtr around first sk
st, pull up 4½-inch lp on hook, turn
hook clockwise 10 times, sl st in top
of last st, sc in next st, rep from *
across. Fasten off.

fringe

poncho doll fringe scarf

SKILL LEVEL

INTERMEDIATE

FINISHED SIZE

5 x 55 inches, including Fringe

MATERIALS

- Brown Sheep Cotton Fleece light (light worsted) weight yarn (3½ oz/ 215 yds/99g per skein):

  2 skeins #CW625 terracotta canyon

  1 skein #CW105 putty
- Size H/8/5mm crochet hook or size needed to obtain gauge
- Cardboard:

  4-inch piece

  3½-inch piece

GAUGE

18 sts = 5 inches; 10 rows = 3 inches

PATTERN NOTES

Post stitches are worked around post of stitches 2 rows below throughout.

Leave stitches behind post stitches unworked.

SPECIAL STITCH

Close single crochet (close sc): Insert hook in **back lp** *(see Stitch Guide)* of sk st 2 rows below, then insert hook in st 1 row below this row, yo, pull through st and back lp, yo, pull through all lps on hook.

INSTRUCTIONS

SCARF

Row 1: With terracotta canyon, ch 19, sc in **back bar** *(see illustration on page 4)* of 2nd ch from hook, and in back bar of each ch across, turn.

Row 2: Ch 1, sc in each st across, turn.

Row 3: Ch 1, sc in first st, *fptr *(see Stitch Guide)* around next st, sc in next st, sk next 2 sts 2 rows below, **fpdtr** *(see Stitch Guide)* around next st, sc in next st, working in front of last post st, fpdtr around first sk st, sc in next st, fptr around next st* sc in each of next 2 sts, rep between *, sc in last st, turn.

Row 4: Rep row 2.

Row 5: Ch 1, sc in first st, *[sk next 2 sts 2 rows below, fpdtr around next st, sc in next st, working in back of last post st, fpdtr in first sk st, sc in next st] twice*, sc in next st, rep between *, turn.

Row 6: Rep row 2.

Row 7: Ch 1, sc in first st, fptr around next st, sc in next st, *sk next 2 sts 2 rows below, fpdtr around next st, sc in next st, working in front of last post st, fpdtr around first sk st*, sc in each of next 2 sts, fptr around next st to right, fptr around st 1 st to left, sc in each of next 2 sc, rep between * once, sc in next st, fptr around next st, sc in last st, turn.

Row 8: Ch 1, sc in each of first 8 sts, **close sc** *(see Special Stitch)* in each of next 2 sts, sc in each of last 8 sts, turn.

Row 9: Ch 1, sc in first st, *sk next 2 sts 2 rows below, fpdtr around next st, sc in next st, working in back of last post st, fpdtr around first sk st, sc in next st*, fptr around next st, sc in each of next 2 sts, sk next st 2 rows below, fpdtr around next st, working in front of last post st, fptr around sk st, sc in each of next 2 sts, fpdtr around next st, sc in next st, rep between * once, turn.

Row 10: Rep row 8.

Row 11: Ch 1, sc in first st, fptr around next st, sc in next st, *sk next 2 sts 2 rows below, fpdtr around next st, sc in next st, working in front of last post st, fpdtr around first sk st*, sc in each of next 2 sts, fptr around each of next 2 sts, sc in each of next 2 sts, rep between * once, sc in next st, fptr around next st, sc in last st, turn.

Rows 12 & 13: Rep rows 8 and 9.

Row 14: Rep row 8.

Row 15: Ch 1, sc in first st, fptr around next st, sc in next st, *sk next 2 sts 2 rows below, fpdtr around next st, sc in next st, working in front of last post st, fpdtr around first sk st*, sc in next st, sk next st 2 rows below, fpdtr around next st, sc in each of next 2 sts, fptr around post st 2 sts to right, sc in next st, rep between * once, sc in next st, fptr around next st, sc in last st, turn.

Row 16: Rep row 2.

Row 17: Rep row 5.

Next rows: Rep rows 2–17 consecutively until piece measures 49 inches from beg, ending with row 3. At end of last row, Fasten off.

Poncho Doll Fringe

Doll

Make 4.

Body

Wrap putty around 4-inch piece of cardboard 30 times.

For **hanger**, cut strand of putty 10 inches long, slide Body off cardboard, insert strand through 1 end of Body lps and tie securely leaving long ends. Cut lps open at other end.

Head

Cut another strand of putty 6 inches long, wrap around Body ¾ inch from top.

Arms

Wrap putty around 3½ inch piece of cardboard 10 times. Slide Arms off cardboard.

fringe

Divide Body in half for front and back, slide Arms between the 2 layers. Cut 10 inch strand of yarn and tie around Body just below Arms to form waist.

Trim Body length to 3 inches. Trim Arms to 2½ inches across. Cut ends of lps on Arms.

Cut 2 strands each 6 inches long. Tie 6-inch strands around ends of Arms for hands.

PONCHO

Make 1 for each Doll.

Row 1: With terracotta canyon, ch 2, sc in back bar of 2nd ch from hook, turn.

Row 2: Ch 1, sc in st, turn.

Rows 3–5: Rep row 2.

Row 6: Ch 1, sc in st, do not turn.

Row 7: Ch 1, sc in left side of last sc, turn.

Rows 8–12: Rep row 2. At end of last row, fasten off.

Sew end of row 1 to end of row 12.

Fringe

Cut 2½-inch strand of terracotta canyon for each Fringe. Fold strand in half, pull fold through, pull ends through fold. Pull to tighten. Evenly sp Fringe around Poncho. Place 1 Poncho on each Doll. Attach 2 Dolls to each end of Scarf as shown in photo.

points

twisted stitches

Background

Row 1 (RS): Ch multiple of 14 chs plus 9, sc in **back bar** *(see illustration on page 4)* of 2nd ch from hook, and in back bar of each ch across, turn.

Row 2: Ch 1, sc in first st, [sc in **front lp** *(see Stitch Guide)* of next st, sc in **back lp** *(see Stitch Guide)* on next st] across to last st, sc in both lps of last st, turn.

Row 3: Rep row 2.

Row 4: Ch 1, *twist work by turning top of work forward and down so the unworked lps of starting ch on row 1 are at the top, sc in both lps of unworked ch, working in unworked chs across, [sc in front lp of next ch, sc in back lp of next ch] 3 times, twist work by turning top of work forward and down so the sts from row 3 are at the top *(you will sk next 7 sts before you continue)*, continuing across row, sc in both lps of next st**, [sc in back lp of next st, sc in front lp of next st] 3 times, rep from * across *(you will be skipping 7 sts before continuing on opposite side)*, ending last rep at **, turn.

Row 5: Rep row 2. Fasten off.

topsy-turvy

Background

Row 1 (RS): Ch multiple of 6 chs plus 1, sc in **back bar** *(see illustration on page 4)* of 2nd ch from hook, and in back bar of each ch across, turn.

Row 2: Ch 1, sc in first st, [sc in **front lp** *(see Stitch Guide)* of next st, sc in **back lp** *(see Stitch Guide)* of next st] across to last st, sc in both lps of last st, turn.

Row 3: Rep row 2.

Row 4: Ch 1, sl st in first st, *[ch 14, sl st in back bar of 2nd ch from hook and in back bar of each ch across, sl st in next st] twice, insert hook in end of first ch just made forming a lp *(keep 2nd ch in back of lp just formed)*, insert hook in next st, yo, pull through st, ch and lp on hook, form lp with 2nd ch by taking it from back to front over first lp, then inserting it through first lp from front to back, insert hook in end of 2nd ch, insert hook in next st, yo, pull through st, ch and lp on hook**, sl st in each of next 2 sts, rep from * across, ending last rep at **, sl st in last st.

Fasten off.

points

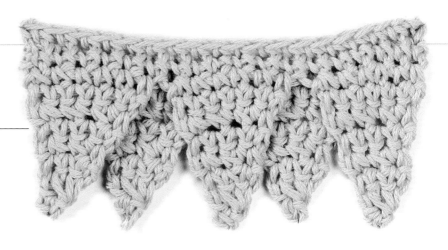

layered points

Background

Row 1 (RS): Ch multiple of 6 chs plus 1, sc in **back bar** *(see illustration on page 4)* of 2nd ch from hook, and in back bar of each ch across, turn.

Row 2: Ch 1, sc in **front lp** *(see Stitch Guide)* of each st across, turn.

Row 3: Ch 1, sc in **back lp** *(see Stitch Guide)* of each st on row 1, turn, join with sl st in first st of row 2.

First Front Point

Row 1 (RS): Working in sts of row 3, ch 1, sc in each of first 6 sts, leaving rem sts unworked, turn.

Row 2: Ch 1, sc in each st across, turn.

Row 3: Ch 1, sc in first st, [**sc dec** *(see Stitch Guide)* in next 2 sts] twice, sc in last st, turn.

Row 4: Rep row 2.

Row 5: Ch 1, sc in first st, sc dec in next 2 sts, sc in last st, turn.

Row 6: Rep row 2.

Row 7: Ch 1, sc dec in 3 sts, turn.

Row 8: Ch 1, sc in sc. Fasten off.

Next Front Point

Row 1: Working in sts of row 3, join with sc in next unworked st, sc in each of next 5 sts, leaving rem sts unworked, turn.

Rows 2–8: Rep rows 2–8 of First Front Point.

Rep Next Front Point across Background.

First Back Point

Row 1: Working in sts of row 2, with WS facing, join with sc in 4th st, sc in each of next 5 sts, leaving rem sts unworked, turn.

Rows 2–8: Rep rows 2–8 of First Front Point.

Next Back Point

Row 1: Working in sts of row 2, join with sc in next unworked st, sc in each of next 5 sts, leaving rem sts unworked, turn.

Rows 2–8: Rep rows 2–8 of First Front Point.

Rep Next Back Point across Background to last 3 sts, leave 3 sts unworked.

ribbed shells

Background

Row 1: Ch any number of chs plus 1, sc in **back bar** *(see illustration on page 4)* of 2nd ch from hook, and in back bar of each ch across, turn.

Row 2: Ch 1, sc in **back lp** *(see Stitch Guide)* of each st across, turn.

Next rows: Rep row 2 to desired length, working multiple of 4 rows plus 1 row. At end of last row, **do not turn.**

Shell row (RS): Working in ends of rows, ch 1, sc in end of first row, [sk next row, 5 dc in next row, sk next row, sc in next row] across. Fasten off.

cabled points

PATTERN NOTES

Post stitches are worked around post
  of stitches 2 rows below throughout.

Leave stitches behind post stitches unworked.

Background

Row 1 (WS): Ch multiple of 4 chs plus 2, sc in **back
bar** *(see illustration on page 4)* of 2nd ch from hook, [sc
in back bar of next ch, ch 8, sk next ch, sc in back bar
of each of next 2 chs] across, sl st in same ch as last
sc, working on opposite side of ch, ch 1, sc in first ch,
[sc in next ch, sc in next ch sp, sc in each of next 2 chs]
across, turn.

Row 2 (RS): Ch 1, sc in first st, [**fpdtr** *(see Stitch
Guide)* around left side of ch-8 sp formed on row 1, sc
in next st, working in back of last post st, fpdtr around
right side of same ch-8 sp, sc in next st] across turn.

Row 3: Ch 1, sc in each st across, turn.

Row 4: Ch 1, sc in first st, [**fptr** *(see Stitch Guide)*
around post of next st, sc in next st] across, turn.

Row 5: Rep row 3.

Row 6: Ch 1, sc in first st, [sk next 2 sts 2 rows below,
fpdtr *(see Stitch Guide)* around post of next st, sc in
next st, working in back of last post st, fpdtr in first sk
st, sc in next st] across. Fasten off.

ribbed points

Background

Row 1: Ch multiple of 7 chs plus 1, sc in **back bar** *(see
illustration on page 4)* of 2nd ch from hook, and in back
bar of each ch across, turn.

Row 2: Ch 1, sc in **back lp** *(see Stitch Guide)* of each st
across to last st, leave last st unworked, turn.

Row 3: Ch 1, sc in back lp of each st across, turn.

Rows 4 & 5: Rep rows 2 and 3.

Row 6: Ch 1, sc in back lp of each st across to last st,
leave last st unworked, ch 2, turn.

Row 7: Sc in back lp of 2nd ch from hook and in back lp
of each st across, turn.

Row 8: Ch 1, sc in back lp of each st across, ch 2, turn.

Rows 9 & 10: Rep rows 7 and 8.

Row 11: Rep row 7.

Next rows: Rep rows 2–11 consecutively to desired
length. At end of last row, fasten off.

points

ants on a log

Background

Row 1 (RS): Ch multiple of 2 chs plus 2, sc in **back bar** *(see illustration on page 4)* of 2nd ch from hook, and in back bar of each ch across, turn.

Row 2: Ch 1, sc in each st across, turn.

Row 3: *Ch 3, dc in 3rd ch from hook, sk next st, sl st in next st, rep from * across. Fasten off.

shelled diamonds

Background

Row 1 (RS): Ch multiple of 4 chs plus 2, sc in **back bar** *(see illustration on page 4)* of 2nd ch from hook, and in back bar of each ch across, turn.

Row 2: Ch 1, sc in each st across, turn.

Row 3: (Ch 3, dc, ch 4, sl st in back bar of 3rd ch from hook, ch 1, 2 dc) in first st, *sk next 3 sts, (2 dc, ch 4, sl st in back bar of 3rd ch from hook, ch 1, 2 dc) in next st, rep from * across. Fasten off.

bubbled bobbles

Background

Row 1 (RS): Ch multiple of 3 chs plus 2, sc in **back bar** *(see illustration on page 4)* of 2nd ch from hook, and in back bar of each ch across, turn.

Row 2: Ch 1, sc in each st across, turn.

Row 3: Ch 1, sc in **front lp** *(see Stitch Guide)* of first st, *sc in **back lp** *(see Stitch Guide)* of same st, **turn**, ch 1, sc in front lp of st just made, sc in back lp of first st made, ch 1, insert hook in first st, yo, pull lp through, insert hook in next st, yo, pull lp through, insert hook in same st on Background as sc, yo, pull through st and all lps on hook**, sl st in each of next 2 sts, sc in front lp of next st, rep from * across, ending last rep at **. Fasten off.

chevron ripples

SPECIAL STITCHES

Beginning double crochet decrease (beg dc dec): Ch 2, sk next st, dc in next st.

Ending double crochet decrease (end dc dec): Holding back last lp of each st on hook, dc in next st, sk next st, dc in next st, yo, pull through all lps on hook.

Double crochet decrease (dc dec): Holding back last lp of each st on hook, dc in next st, sk next 3 sts, dc in next st, yo, pull through all lps on hook.

Beginning treble crochet decrease (beg tr dec): Ch 3, sk next st, tr in next st.

Ending treble crochet decrease (end tr dec): Holding back last lp of each st on hook, tr in next st, sk next 3 sts, tr in next st, yo, pull through all lps on hook.

Treble crochet decrease (tr dec): Holding back last lp of each st on hook, tr in next st, sk next st, tr in next st, yo, pull through all sts on hook.

Background

Row 1 (RS): Ch multiple of 16 chs plus 2, dc in **back bar** *(see illustration on page 4)* of 4th ch from hook *(first 3 chs and dc count as first dc dec)*, [dc in back bar of each of next 5 chs, (dc ch 3, dc) in back bar of next ch, dc in back bar of each of next 5 chs**, **dc dec** *(see Special Stitches)*, rep from * across, ending last rep at **, **end dc dec** *(see Special Stitches)*, turn.

Row 2: Beg dc dec *(see Special Stitches)*, *dc in each of next 4 sts, (2 dc, ch 3, 2 dc) in next ch-3 sp, dc in each of next 4 sts**, dc dec, rep from * across, ending last rep at **, ending dc dec, turn.

Row 3: Rep row 2.

Row 4: Beg tr dec *(see Special Stitches)*, *dc in each of next 2 sts, hdc in each of next 2 sts, (2 sc, ch 2, 2 sc) in next ch sp, hdc in each of next 2 sts, dc in each of next 2 sts**, **tr dec** *(see Special Stitches)*, rep from * across, ending last rep at **, **end tr dec** *(see Special Stitches)*, turn.

Row 5: Beg tr dec, *dc in each of next 2 sts, hdc in each of next 2 sts, 2 sc in next ch sp, hdc in each of next 2 sts, dc in each of next 2 sts**, tr dec, rep from * across, ending last rep at **, ending tr dec, turn.

Row 6: Ch 1, sc in each st across, turn.

Row 7: Rep row 6. Fasten off.

points

rolled points

Background

Row 1: Ch 3, sc in **back bar** *(see illustration on page 4)* of 2nd ch from hook, and in back bar of last ch, turn.

Row 2: Ch 1, sc in first st, 2 sc in last st, turn.

Row 3: Ch 1, 2 sc in first st, sc in each st across, turn.

Row 4: Ch 1, sc in each of first 3 sts, 2 sc in last st, ch 6, turn.

Row 5: Sc in back bar of 2nd ch from hook and in back bar of each ch across, sc in each st across, turn.

Row 6: Ch 1, sc in each of first 3 sts, **sc dec** *(see Stitch Guide)* in next 2 sts, leaving rem sts unworked, turn.

Row 7: Ch 1, sc dec in first 2 sts, sc in each of last 2 sts, turn.

Row 8: Ch 1, sc in first st, sc dec in last 2 sts, turn.

Row 9: Ch 1, sc in each st across, turn.

Next rows: Rep rows 2–9 consecutively to desired length, ending with row 9. At end of last row, **do not turn.**

Last row: Working in ends of rows, ch 1, evenly sp sc across. Fasten off.

Roll each point up in ball, sew ball in place.

diagonal points

Background

Row 1: Ch any number of chs plus 1, sc in **back bar** *(see illustration on page 4)* of 2nd ch from hook, and in back bar of each ch across, ch 3, turn.

Row 2: Sc in back bar of 2nd ch from hook, sc in back bar of next ch, sc in each st across, leaving last st unworked, turn.

Row 3: Ch 1, sc in each st across, ch 3, leaving last st unworked, turn.

Next rows: Rep rows 2 and 3 alternately to desired length ending with row 2. At end of last row, **do not turn.**

Last row: Working in ends of rows across side, ch 1, sc in end of each row across. Fasten off.

picot points

Background

Row 1 (RS): Ch any number of chs plus 1, sc in **back bar** *(see illustration on page 4)* of 2nd ch from hook, and in back bar of each ch across, turn.

Row 2: Ch 1, sc in each st across, turn.

Row 3: Ch 1, sc in first st, *ch 3, sl st in back bar of 3rd ch from hook**, sc in each of next 2 sts, rep from * across, ending last rep at **, sc in last st. Fasten off.

tiny teeth

Background

Row 1 (RS): Ch any number of chs plus 1, sc in **back bar** *(see illustration on page 4)* of 2nd ch from hook, and in back bar of each ch across, **do not turn.**

Row 2: Ch 1, working from left to right, **reverse sc** *(see illustration on page 39)* in each st across. Fasten off.

hills & valleys

Background

Row 1 (RS): Ch multiple of 7 chs plus 1, sc in **back bar** *(see illustration on page 4)* of 2nd ch from hook, and in back bar of each ch across, turn.

Row 2: Ch 1, sc in each st across, turn.

Rows 3–5: Rep row 2.

Row 6: Ch 1, sc in each of first 2 sts, *hdc in next st, yo, insert hook in next st, yo, pull lp through, tightly wrap yarn from front to back around Background, [yo, pull through 2 lps on hook] twice, hdc in next st**, sc in each of next 4 sts, rep from * across, ending last rep at **, sc in each of last 2 sts, turn.

Row 7: Rep row 2. Fasten off.

points

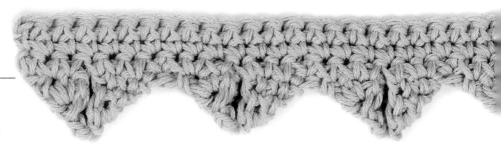

mountain peaks

Background

Row 1: Ch 4, sc in **back bar** *(see illustration on page 4)* of 2nd ch from hook, and in back bar of each ch across, turn.

Row 2: Ch 1, sc in each st across, turn.

Rows 3–7: Rep row 2.

Row 8: Ch 1, sc in first st, ch 3, leaving rem sts unworked, turn.

Row 9: Sc in back bar of 2nd ch from hook and back bar of next ch, sc in last st, turn.

Rows 10–15: Rep row 2.

Next rows: Rep rows 8–15 consecutively to desired length, ending with row 15. At end of last row, **do not turn.**

Edging

Row 1 (RS): Ch 1, *fold ends of rectangle below up to back of work so sides of rectangle are at top and even with this row and triangle is formed, working through all thicknesses, evenly sp 6 sc across triangle**, sc in end of next row, rep from * across, ending last rep at **, turn.

Row 2: Ch 1, sc in each st across, turn.

Row 3: Rep row 2. Fasten off.

rolling waves

Background

Row 1 (RS): Ch multiple of 6 chs plus 2, sc in **back bar** *(see illustration on page 4)* of 2nd ch from hook, and in back bar of each ch across, turn.

Row 2: Ch 1, sc in each st across, turn.

Row 3: Ch 1, sc in first st, *ch 1, insert hook in vertical lp on side of last st, yo, pull lp through, insert hook in next st, yo, pull lp through, [yo, pull through 2 lps on hook] twice, ch 1, insert hook in first vertical lp on side of last st, yo, pull lp through, insert hook in next vertical lp on side of same st, yo, pull lp through, insert hook in next st on this row, yo, pull lp through, [yo, pull through 2 lps on hook] 3 times, ch 1, insert hook in first vertical lp on side of last st, yo, pull lp through, [insert hook in next vertical lp on side of same st, yo, pull lp through] twice, insert hook in next st on this row, yo, pull lp through, [yo, pull through 2 lps on hook] 4 times, ch 1, sk first 2 vertical lps on side of last st, [insert hook in next vertical lp on side of last st, yo, pull lp through] twice, insert hook in next st on this row, yo, pull lp though, [yo, pull through 2 lps on hook] 3 times, ch 1, sk first 2 vertical lps on side of last st, insert hook in next vertical lp on side of last st, yo, pull lp through, insert hook in next st on this row, yo, pull lp through, [yo, pull through 2 lps on hook] twice, ch 1, sc in next st, rep from * across. Fasten off.

twisted stitch rope purse

SKILL LEVEL

INTERMEDIATE

FINISHED SIZE

1½ x 7 x 9 inches, excluding Strap

MATERIALS

- Brown Sheep Cotton Fleece light (light worsted) weight yarn (3½ oz/ 215 yds/99g per skein):
    2 skeins #CW725 buttercream
- Size H/8/5mm crochet hook or size needed to obtain gauge
- Tapestry needle
- Sewing needle
- Sewing thread to match
- Fabric for lining:
    2 pieces 1¾ x 6½
    14½ x 9 inches
- Snap
- 6mm eyelet: 2
- Elastic: 2 pieces 3 inches long

GAUGE

8 sts = 2 inches; 7 rows = 2 inches

points

INSTRUCTIONS

PURSE

Side
Make 2.

Row 1: Ch 37, sc in **back bar** *(see illustration on page 4)* of 2nd ch from hook, and in back bar of each ch across, turn. *(36 sc)*

Note: Working sc in back bar of ch will leave 2 lps of the ch which will be used on row 4.

Row 2: Ch 1, sc in first st, [sc in **front lp** *(see Stitch Guide)* of next st, sc in **back lp** *(see Stitch Guide)* of next st] across to last st, sc in both lps of last st, turn.

Row 3: Rep row 2.

Row 4: Ch 1, twist work by turning top of work forward and down so unused lps of starting ch on row 1 are at the top, *sc in both lps of ch, working in ch across, [sc in front lp of next ch, sc in back lp of next ch] 3 times, twist work by turning top of work forward and down so the sts from row 3 are at the top, sk 7 sts before continuing across row, sc in both lps of next st**, [sc in back lp of next st, sc in front lp of next st] 3 times, twist work by turning top of work forward and down so unused lps of starting ch on row 1 are at the top, sk 7 chs before continuing, rep from * across, ending last rep at **, turn.

Row 5: Ch 1, sc in back lp of each st across, turn.

Note: Rows 1–4 will be turned down for Trim.

Rows 6–30: Rep row 2. At end of last row, fasten off. Piece should measure 9 inches wide.

End
Make 2.

Row 1: Ch 6, sc in back bar of 2nd ch from hook, and in back bar of each ch across, turn. *(5 sc)*

Row 2: Ch 1, sc in first st, sc in front lp of next st, sc in back lp of next st, sc in front lp of next st, sc in both lps of last st, turn. This is the top edge.

Row 3: Ch 1, sc in each of first 2 sts, ch 1, sk next st, sc in each of next 2 sts, turn.

Row 4: Ch 1, sc in first st, sc in front lp of next st, sc in ch sp, sc in front lp of next st, sc in last st, turn.

Row 5: Ch 1, sc in first st, sc in back lp of next st, sc in front lp of next st, sc in back lp of next st, sc in last st, turn.

Row 6: Rep row 2.

Rows 7–26: Rep rows 5 and 6 alternately. At end of last row, fasten off.

Bottom

Row 1: Ch 6, sc in back bar of 2nd ch from hook, and in back bar of each ch across, turn. *(5 sc)*

Row 2: Ch 1, sc in each st across, turn.

Next rows: Rep row 2 until piece measures 9 inches from beg. At end of last row, fasten off.

Pocket
Make 2.
Trim

Row 1 (RS): Ch 16, sc in back bar of 2nd ch from hook, and in back bar of each ch across, turn. *(15 sc)*

Row 2: Ch 1, sc in first st, [sc in front lp of next st, sc in back lp of next st] across to last 2 sts, sc in back lp of next st, sc in both lps of last st, turn.

Row 3: Ch 1, sc in first st, [sc back lp of next st, sc in back lp of next st] across to last 2 sts, sc in front lp of next st, sc in both lps of last st, turn.

Row 4: Ch 1, twist work by turning top of work forward and down so unused lps of starting ch on row 1 are at the top, sc in both lps of 1 ch, working in ch across [sc in front lp of next ch, sc in back lp of next ch] 3 times, twist work by turning top of work forward and down so the sts for row 3 are at the top, sk 7 sts before continuing across row, sc in both lps of next st, [sc in back lp of next st, sc in front lp of next st] 3 times, twist work by turning top of work forward and down so unused lps of starting ch on row 1 are at the top, sk next 7 chs, sc in both lps of last ch, turn.

Body

Row 5: Ch 1, sc in back of each st across, turn.

Rows 6–17: Rep rows 2 and 3 alternately. At end of last row, fasten off.

Edging

With RS facing, join with sc on row 5 of Pocket, evenly sp sc down side, ch 1 for corner, evenly sp sc across bottom edge, ch 1 for corner, evenly sp sc up next side to other end of row 5. Leaving long end, fasten off.

Assembly

With sewing needle and thread, sew ends of 3-inch piece of elastic to ends of row 5 on Pocket Body so elastic is between Pocket Body and Trim when Trim is turned down. Elastic length is smaller than Pocket width so Pocket will gather slightly. Fold Trim down and sew in place to Body covering elastic.

Sew Pockets on front Side piece, placing bottom of Pockets on row 28 of front.

ASSEMBLY

1. Fold rows 1–4 down on each side to form trim. Sew in place.

2. With RS facing, sew bottom edge of front Side to Bottom. Sew bottom edge of back Side to Bottom. Seams will be on inside of Purse.

3. With RS facing and top edges of End at top, sc to side edge of front Side, Bottom and back Side. Rep on other side edge with rem End.

4. Fold 14½ x 9-inch fabric in half to make a 7¼ x 9-inch rectangle. Sew 1¾ x 6½-inch fabric pieces to sides for end gussets, leaving 9-inch opening at top. Fold over ½-inch hem to outside of lining; stitch in place. Place lining inside Purse. Make a small hole at each end of

lining to match the ch-1 sp on row 3 of Ends.

5. Place 1 eyelet in each hole on each End.

6. Sew snap in top opening or zipper may be used.

7. Sew top edge of lining to front and back Sides.

STRAP

Cut 4 strands of yarn 175 inches long. Holding all strands tog, fold in half. Tie ends in knot.

Place knotted end onto stationary object the diameter of a pencil. Place folded end on finger. Pull strands taut. Twist strands 87 times. Place 1 finger in center of strands, fold in half letting strands twist tog forming rope Strap.

Insert 1 end of Strap through each eyelet on Purse, tie knot 3 inches from end on each end of Strap to secure and form tassel. Trim tassel as desired.

points

ruffles

fancy ribs

Background

Row 1 (RS): Ch 8, sc in **back bar** *(see illustration on page 4)* of 2nd ch from hook, and in back bar of each ch across, turn.

Row 2: Ch 1, sc in **back bar** *(see illustration)* of each st across, turn.

Back Bar of Single Crochet

Next rows: Rep row 2 to desired length, working an even number of rows. At end of last row, **do not turn.**

Edging

Row 1 (RS): Working in ends of rows, ch 1, sc in end of first row, [sc in end of next row which has vertical lps] across, sc in end of last row, there should be half as many sts plus 1 as number of rows on Ruffle

Row 2: Ch 1, sc in each st across, turn.

Row 3: Rep row 2. Fasten off.

fancy frills

Background

Row 1 (RS): Ch even number of chs plus 1, hdc in **back bar** *(see illustration on page 4)* of 3rd ch from hook *(first 2 chs count as first hdc)*, and in back bar of each ch across, turn.

Row 2: Ch 2 *(counts as first hdc)*, working around post of sts 1 row below, [**fpdc** *(see Stitch Guide)* around next st, **bpdc** *(see Stitch Guide)* around next st] across to last st, hdc in last st, turn.

Rows 3 & 4: Rep row 2.

Row 5: Ch 4 *(counts as first hdc and ch-1)*, dc in same st, (ch 1, dc) twice in next st and in each st across. Fasten off.

pretty frilly

Background

Row 1 (RS): Ch any number of chs plus 1, sc in **back bar** *(see illustration on page 4)* of 2nd ch from hook, and in back bar of each ch across, turn.

Row 2: Ch 1, sc in each st across, turn.

Row 3: Ch 1, (sc, ch 3, sc) in first st, [ch 3, (sc, ch 3, sc) in next st] across, turn.

Row 4: Sl st in first ch-3 sp, ch 1, (sc, ch 3, sc) in same ch sp, [ch 3, (sc, ch 3, sc) in next ch sp] across. Fasten off.

ruffles

traditional ruffle

Background

Row 1 (RS): Ch 12, sc in **back bar** *(see illustration on page 4)* of 2nd ch from hook, sc in back bar of each of next 2 chs, dc in back bar of each of last 8 chs, turn.

Row 2: Ch 3 *(counts as first dc)*, dc in **front lp** *(see Stitch Guide)* of each st across to last 3 sts, sc in both lps of next st, dc in both lps of next st, sc in both lps of last st, turn.

Row 3: Ch 1, sc in each of first 3 sts, dc in front lp of each st across to last st, dc in both lps of last st, turn.

Next rows: Rep rows 2 and 3 alternately to desired length, ending with row 2. At end of last row, fasten off.

little frills

SPECIAL STITCH

Surface stitch (surface st): Holding yarn at back of work, insert hook between rows, yo, pull lp through st and lp on hook.

Background

Row 1: Ch 8, sc in **back bar** *(see illustration on page 4)* of 2nd ch from hook *(mark this as st No. 2)*, sc in back bar of next ch *(mark this as st No. 4)*, sc in back bar of each ch across, turn.

Row 2: Ch 1, sc in each st across, turn.

Next rows: Rep row 2 to desired length, working in multiple of 6 rows plus 1.

Last row: Ch 1, sc in each of first 5 sts, sc in next st *(mark this as st No. 3)*, sc in last st *(mark this as st No. 1)*, do not turn.

Edging

Working in ends of rows, ch 1, sc in end of each row across. Fasten off.

Surface Stitch Ruffle

Row 1: Surface st *(see Special Stitches)* in st No. 1, surface st across rows to st No. 2, surface st in next row, *insert hook from front to back through next row, sk next row, insert hook from back to front through next row, sk next row, insert hook from front to back through next row, yo, pull through all rows and lp on hook, surface st in next row, rep from * across. Fasten off.

Row 2: Using the same procedure as established in row 1, work surface sts from No. 3 to No. 4.

rows of ruffles

Background

Row 1 (RS): Ch any number of chs plus 1, sc in **back bar** *(see illustration on page 4)* of 2nd ch from hook, and in back bar of each ch across, turn.

Row 2: Ch 1, sc in each st across, turn.

Row 3: Rep row 2.

Row 4a: Working in **front lps** *(see Stitch Guide)*, ch 1, sc in each st across, turn.

Row 4b: Working in **back lps** *(see Stitch Guide)* of row 3, 3 sc in each st across, join with sl st in beg sc of row 4a.

Row 5 (WS): Ch 1, sc in each st across row 4a, turn.

Row 6a: Working in front lps, ch 1, sc in each st across, turn.

Row 6b: Working in back lps of row 5, 3 sc in each st across, join with sl st in beg sc on row 6a, turn.

Row 7 (RS): Ch 1, sc in each st across row 6b, turn.

Rows 8–11: Rep rows 4a–7. At end of last row, fasten off.

box pleats

Background

Row 1 (RS): Ch multiple of 6 chs plus 5, sc in **back bar** *(see illustration on page 4)* of 2nd ch from hook, and in back bar of each ch across, turn.

Row 2a: Ch 1, sc in **front lp** *(see Stitch Guide)* of each st across, turn.

Row 2b: Sc in **back lps** *(see Stitch Guide)* of each st on row 1 across, turn.

Row 3: Ch 1, sc in first st of row 2a and row 2b at same time, sc in next st of row 2a and row 2b at same time, *sc in front lp of each of next 3 sts on row 2a, **turn,** working in unworked lps of row 2a and back lps of 2b at same time, sc in each of next 3 sts, **turn,** working in rem lps of row 2b, sc in each of next 3 sts, [sc in next st on row 2a, and next st on row 2b at same st] twice, rep from * across, turn.

Row 4: Ch 1, sc in first st, [sc in front lp of next st, sc in back lp of next st] across to last st, sc in both lps of last st, turn.

Next row: Rep row 4 to desired length. At end of last row, fasten off.

ruffles

baby bells

PATTERN NOTES

Post stitches are worked around post of stitch 2 rows below throughout. Leave stitches behind post stitches unworked.

Background

Row 1 (RS): Ch odd number of chs plus 1, sc in **back bar** *(see illustration on page 4)* of 2nd ch from hook, and in back bar of each ch across, turn.

Row 2: Ch 1, sc in each st across, turn.

Row 3: Ch 1, sc in first st, [**fptr** *(see Stitch Guide)* around next st, sc in next st] across, turn.

Row 4: Ch 1, sc in first st, [3 sc in next st, sc in next st] across, turn.

Row 5: Ch 1, sc in each of first 2 sts, *3 sc in next st**, sc in each of next 3 sts, rep from * across, ending last rep at **, sc in each of last 2 sts, turn.

Row 6: Ch 1, sc in first st, [ch 1, sk next 5 sts, sc in next st] across. Fasten off.

ribs & bells

PATTERN NOTES

Work post stitches as post of stitch 1 row below throughout. Leave stitch behind post stitch unworked.

Background

Row 1 (WS): Ch multiple of 6 chs plus 6, hdc in **back bar** *(see illustration on page 4)* of 3rd ch from hook *(first 2 chs count as first hdc)*, and in back bar of each ch across, turn.

Row 2: Ch 2 *(counts as first hdc)*, [**fpdc** *(see Stitch Guide)* around post of next st, **bpdc** *(see Stitch Guide)* around post of next st] across to last 2 sts, fpdc around post of next st, hdc in last st, turn.

Row 3: Ch 2, [bpdc around next st, fpdc around next st] across to last 2 sts, bpdc around next st, hdc in last st, turn.

Row 4: Ch 2, *[fpdc around next st, bpdc around next st] twice, ch 1, 3 hdc in next st, ch 1, bpdc around next st, rep from * across to last 4 sts, fpdc around next st, bpdc around next st, fpdc around next st, hdc in last st, turn.

Row 5: Ch 2, *[bpdc around next st fpdc around next st] twice, ch 1, hdc in next ch sp, hdc in each of next 3 sts, hdc in next ch sp, ch 1, fpdc around next st, rep from * across to last 4 sts, bpdc around next st, fpdc around next st, bpdc around next st, hdc in last st, turn.

Row 6: Ch 2, *[fpdc around next st, bpdc around next st] twice, ch 1, hdc in next ch sp, hdc in each of next 5 sts, hdc in next ch sp, ch 1, bpdc around next st, rep from * across to last 4 sts, fpdc around next st, bpdc around next st, fpdc around next st, hdc in last st, turn.

Row 7: Ch 2, *[bpdc around next st, fpdc around next st] twice, ch 1, hdc in next ch sp, hdc in each of next 7 sts, hdc in next ch sp, ch 1, fpdc around next st, rep from * across to last 4 sts, bpdc around next st, fpdc around next st, bpdc around next st, hdc in last st. Fasten off.

double trouble

Background

Row 1: Ch multiple of 3 chs plus 1, sc in **back bar** *(see illustration on page 4)* of 2nd ch from hook, and in back bar of each ch across, turn.

Row 2: Ch 1, sc in each st across, turn.

First Layer

Row 1: Ch 1, sc in **front lp** *(see Stitch Guide)* of first st, *ch 1, (sc, ch 1, sc) in front lp of next st, ch 1**, sc in front lp of each of next 2 sts, rep from * across, ending last rep at **, sc in front lp of last st, turn.

Row 2: Ch 1, sc in first st, *ch 1, sk next ch-1 sp, sc in next sc, ch 1, sc in next ch-1 sp, ch 1, sc in next sc, ch 1, sk next ch-1 sp**, sc in each of next 2 sc, rep from * across, ending last rep at **, sc in last st, turn.

Row 3: Ch 1, sc in first st, *ch 1, sk next ch-1 sp, sc in next sc, ch 1, sc in next ch-1 sp, ch 1, sk next sc, sc in next ch-1 sp, ch 1, sc in next sc, ch 1, sk next ch-1 sp**, sc in each of next 2 sc, rep from * across, ending last rep at **, sc in last st. Fasten off.

2nd Layer Ruffle

Row 1 (RS): With RS facing, join with sc in unworked lp of row 2, sc in each unworked lp across, turn.

Rows 2–4: Ch 1, sc in each st across, turn.

Row 5: Ch 1, sc in first st, *ch 1, (sc, ch 1, sc) in next st, ch 1**, sc in each of next 2 sts, rep from * across, ending last rep at **, sc in last st, turn.

Rows 6 & 7: Rep rows 2 and 3 of First Layer Ruffle. Fasten off.

pretty bitty bows

Background

Row 1: Ch multiple of 5 chs plus 1, sc in **back bar** *(see illustration on page 4)* of 2nd ch from hook, and in back bar of each ch across, turn.

Row 2: Ch 1, sc in each st across, turn.

First Ruffle

Row 1: Ch 1, sc in first st, [ch 3, sc in next st] 4 times, leaving rem sts unworked, turn.

Row 2: Ch 1, sc in first ch-3 sp, [ch 3, sc in next ch-3 sp] 3 times, turn.

Row 3: Ch 1, sc in first ch-3 sp, [ch 3, sc in next ch-3 sp] twice, turn.

Row 4: Ch 1, sc in first ch-3 sp, ch 3, sc in last ch-3 sp. Fasten off.

Next Ruffle

Row 1: Join with sc in next unworked st on row 2 of Background, [ch 3, sc in next st] 4 times, leaving rem sts unworked, turn.

Rows 2–4: Rep rows 2–4 of First Ruffle.

Rep Next Ruffle across until all sts are used.

Bow

Cut 12-inch strands of contrasting color, cutting 1 more strand than number of Ruffles.

Tie strands into bows connecting Ruffles tog through ch-3 sps on row 1 of Ruffles. Tie 1 strand in bow around row 1 at each end of Ruffles.

ruffles

jagged edges

Background

Row 1 (RS): Ch multiple of 8 chs plus 2, sc in **back bar** *(see illustration on page 4)* of 2nd ch from hook, dc in back bar of next ch, [sc in back bar of next ch, dc in back bar of next ch] across, turn.

Row 2: Ch 1, sc in first st, dc in next st, [sc in next st, dc in next st] across to last st, dc in last st, turn.

Beginning Flap

Row 1: Ch 1, sc in first st, [sc in **front lp** *(see Stitch Guide)* of next st, dc in front lp of next st] twice, leaving rem sts unworked, turn.

Row 2: Ch 1, sc in first st, dc in next st, sc in next st, dc in each of last 2 sts, turn.

Row 3: Ch 1, sc in first st, [sc in next st, dc in next st] twice, turn. Fasten off.

Flap

Row 1: Working in unworked lps on row 2 of Background behind last Flap, join with sc in next st, dc in next st, sc in next st, dc in next st, [sc in next front lp of next st, dc in front lp of next st] twice, leaving rem sts unworked, turn.

Row 2: Ch 1, sc in first st, dc in next st, [sc in next st, dc in next st] across, turn.

Row 3: Rep row 2. Fasten off.

Rep Flap across row 2 of Background to last 4 sts.

End Flap

Row 1: Working in unworked lps on row 2 of Background behind last Flap, join with sc in next st, dc in next st, sc in next st, dc in next st, working in both lps, [sc in next st, dc in next st] across, turn.

Rows 2 & 3: Rep rows 2 and 3 of Flap.

loopy lace

PATTERN NOTE

Design requires 2 hooks; 1 should be 1 size larger than the other.

Background

Row 1 (RS): With small hook, ch any number of chs plus 1, sc in **back bar** *(see illustration on page 4)* of 2nd ch from hook, and in back bar of each ch across, turn.

Row 2: Ch 1, sc in each st across, turn.

Row 3: With larger hook, rep row 2.

Row 4: With larger hook, ch 1, sc in first st, [sc in **front lp** *(see Stitch Guide)* of next st, sc in **back lp** *(see Stitch Guide)* of same st] across to last st, sc in both lps of last st, turn.

Row 5: Ch 1, sc in first st, [sc in front lp of next st, sc in back lp of next st] across to last st, sc in both lps on last st, turn.

Next rows: Rep row 5 to desired length. At end of last row, fasten off.

running ribbons

Background

Row 1 (RS): Ch 6, sc in **back bar** *(see illustration on page 4)* of 2nd ch from hook, and in back bar of each ch across, turn.

Row 2: Ch 1, sc in **front lp** *(see Stitch Guide)* of each st across, turn.

Row 3 (RS): Ch 1, sc in **back lp** *(see Stitch Guide)* of each st across, turn.

Next rows: Rep rows 2 and 3 alternately to desired length ending with row 3. At end of last row, **do not turn**.

Ruffle

Note: *Ruffle will be worked in unworked lps on RS of work.*

Row 1 (RS): Turn work clockwise, then turn work upside down so the RS of work is facing, sc in each unworked lp on row above, turn work counterclockwise, sc in each unworked lp on row below, rep from * across, turn work counterclockwise.

Row 2: Ch 1, sc in each st across. Fasten off.

mini ruffles

SPECIAL STITCH

Back slip stitch (back sl st): Bring yarn to front of work, insert hook in indicated st from back to front so hook is facing down, yarn should be to right of hook, move yarn to left going over hook, then move yarn to right going under hook thereby catching yarn in hook, pull yarn through st and lp on hook, turning hook counterclockwise so the hook is now facing up.

Background

Row 1: Ch 7, **back sl st** *(see Special Stitch)* in **back bar** *(see illustration on page 4)* of 2nd ch from hook, and in back bar of each ch across, turn.

Note: *When working back sl st over a back sl st in previous row the top horizontal lp will be the front lp of the st.*

Row 2: Ch 1, back sl st in **back lp** *(see Stitch Guide)* of each st across *(this will be the horizontal lp at the very top of the st)*, turn.

Row 3: Rep row 2.

Row 4: Ch 1, sl st in back lp in each of first 2 sts, leaving rem sts unworked, turn.

Row 5: Ch 1, back sl st in **front lp** *(see Stitch Guide)* of each st across, turn.

Row 6: Ch 1, sl st in back lp of each st across, sl st in back lp of next st 3 rows below, turn.

Row 7: Rep row 5.

Row 8: Ch 1, sl st in back lp of each st across, back sl st in back lp of next st 5 rows below, back sl st in back lp of each of next 2 sts, turn.

Row 9: Ch 1, back sl st in back lp of each of next 3 sts, back lp st in front lp of each of next 3 sts, turn.

Next rows: Rep rows 2–9 consecutively to desired length, ending with row 2. At end of last row, **do not turn.**

Last row: Working in ends of rows, ch 1, sl st in end of each row across. Fasten off.

ruffles

post stitch ruffle

PATTERN NOTES

Post stitches are worked around post of stitch 2 rows below throughout. Leave stitches behind post stitches unworked.

Background

Row 1 (RS): Ch multiple of 3 chs plus 1, sc in **back bar** *(see illustration on page 4)* of 2nd ch from hook, and in back bar of each ch across, turn.

Row 2: Ch 1, sc in each st across, turn.

Rows 3 & 4: Rep row 2.

Row 5: Ch 1, sc in first st, *5 **fpdc** *(see Stitch Guide)* around next st, sc in each of next 2 sts, rep from * across, ending last rep at **, sc in last st. Fasten off.

laced chains

Background

Row 1 (RS): Ch a multiple of 8 chs plus 6, sc in **back bar** *(see illustration on page 4)* of 2nd ch from hook, and in back bar of each ch across, turn.

Row 2: Ch 1, sc in each st across, turn.

Ruffle

Row 1a: Ch 1, sc in first st, ch 5, sk next st, sc in next st, [ch 7, sk next 3 sts, sc in next st] across to last 2 sts, ch 5, sk next st, sc in last st, turn.

Row 1b: Ch 1, with ch-5 lp in back of work, sc in first sk st, [ch 7, with ch-7 lp in front of work, sc in center sk st of next 3 sk sts, ch 7, with ch-7 lp in back of work, sc in center sk st of next 3 sk sts] across to last 2 sts, ch 5, with ch-5 lp in front of work, sc in last sk st. Fasten off.

gathered ruffles

Background

Row 1: Ch 12, sc in **back bar** *(see illustration on page 4)* of 2nd ch from hook, [ch 1, sk next ch, sc in back bar of next ch] across, turn.

Row 2: Ch 1, sc in first st, [ch 1, sk next ch sp, sc in next st] across, turn.

Next rows: Rep row 2 to desired length working an odd number of rows. At end of last row, fasten off.

Gathering

Turn rows sideways, using tapestry needle, weave strand of yarn through top horizontal rows of ch-1 sps then weave through next row of ch-1 sp directly underneath, pull strand to gather up rows, secure ends.

braided peaks

PATTERN NOTES

Leave stitches behind Front Post Long
   Single Crochet unworked.

SPECIAL STITCH

**Front post long single crochet (fp
long sc):** Insert hook around post
of st 2 rows below, yo, pull lp
through and up even with
this row, yo, pull through all
lps on hook.

Background

Row 1 (RS): Ch multiple of 10
chs plus 10, sc in **back bar** *(see
illustration on page 4)* of 2nd ch from
hook, and in back bar of each ch
across, turn.

Row 2: Ch 1, sc in first st, [sc in
front lp *(see Stitch Guide)* of next
st, sc in **back lp** *(see Stitch Guide)*
of next st] across to last 2 sts, sc in
front lp of next st, sc in both lps of
last st, turn.

Row 3: Ch 1, sc in first st, sc in front
lp of next st, sc in back lp of next st,

sc in front lp of next st, **fp long sc**
(see Special Stitch) around next st,
*[sc in front lp of next st, sc in back
lp of next st] 4 times, sc in front lp of
next st, fp long sc around next st, rep
from * across to last 4 sts, sc in front
lp of next st, sc in back lp of next st,
sc in front lp of next st, sc in both lps
of last st, turn.

Row 4: Ch 1, sc in first st, sc in front
lp of next st, sc in back lp of next st,
*[sk next st, sc in back lp of next st]
twice**, [sc in front lp of next st,
sc in back lp of next st] 3 times, rep
from * across, ending last rep at **,
sc in front lp of next st, sc in both lps
of last st, turn.

Row 5: Ch 1, sc in first st, sc in front
lp of next st, sc in back lp of next
st, fp long sc around next st, *[sc in
back lp of next st, sc in front lp of
next st] 3 times, sc back lp of next st,
fp long sc around next st, rep from *
across to last 3 sts, sc back lp in next
st, sc in front lp in next st, sc in both
lps of last st, turn.

Row 6: Ch 1, sc in first st, sc in front

lp of next st, *[sk next st, sc in front
lp of next st] twice**, [sc in back lp of
next st, sc in front lp of next st] twice,
rep from * across, ending last rep at
**, sc in both lps of last st, turn.

Row 7: Ch 1, sc in first st, sc in front
lp of next st, fp long sc around next
st, *[sc in front lp of next st, sc in
back lp of next st] twice, sc in front
lp of next st, fp long sc around next
st, rep from * across, to last 2 sts, sc
in front lp of next st, sc in both lps of
last st, turn.

Row 8: Ch 1, sc in first st, *[sk next
st, sc in back lp of next st] twice, sc
in front lp of next st, sc in back lp of
next st, rep from * across to last 4
sts, sk next st, sc in back lp of next
st, sk next st, sc in both lps of last
st, turn.

Row 9: Ch 1, sc in first st, fp long sc
around next st, *sc in back lp of next
st, sc in front lp of next st, sc in back
lp of next st, fp long sc around next
st, rep from * across to last st, sc in
both lps of last st, turn.

Row 10: Rep row 2. Fasten off.

ruffles

eyelet ruffles

Background

Row 1 (RS): Ch a multiple of 6 chs plus 3, sc in **back bar** *(see illustration on page 4)* of 2nd ch from hook, and in back bar of each ch across, turn.

Row 2: Ch 1, sc in each st across, turn.

Row 3: Rep row 2.

Row 4: Ch 1, sc in each of first 2 sts, [sk next 4 sts, sc in next st, push sk sts to back of work, sc in next st] across to last st, sc in last st, turn.

Row 5 (RS): Ch 1, sc in first st, [sk first sk st 2 rows below, insert hook in **front lp** *(see Stitch Guide)* of next sk st, *insert hook in both lps of next st 1 row below, yo, pull through st and lp on hook, yo, pull through all lps on hook*, insert hook in front lp of next sk st 2 rows below, rep between * once] across to last st, sc in last st, turn. Fasten off.

This design creates a natural eyelet in row 2 at front of each ruffle. If desired, push end of crochet hook through each opening on row 2 to open eyelet more fully.

peek-a-boo ruffle

PATTERN NOTES

Post stitches are worked around post of stitch 4 rows below throughout.

Leave stitches behind post stitches unworked.

Background

Row 1 (RS): Ch 10, sc in **back bar** *(see illustration on page 4)* of 2nd ch from hook, and in back bar of each ch across, turn.

Row 2: Ch 1, sc in first st, [sc in **front lp** *(see Stitch Guide)* of next st, sc in **back lp** *(see Stitch Guide)* of next st] 3 times, sc in front lp of next st, sc in both lps of last st, turn.

Rows 3–5: Rep row 2.

Row 6: Ch 1, sc in first st, [**fpdc** *(see Stitch Guide)* around post of next st 2 rows below, sc in next st] across, turn.

Rows 7–11: Rep row 2.

Row 12: Rep row 6.

Next rows: Rep rows 2–12 consecutively to desired length, ending with row 12.

Last row: Rep row 2, **do not turn.**

Edging

Row 1: With RS facing and working in ends of rows, ch 1, sc in end of first row, [ch 2, sk ends of next 5 rows, sc in end of next row *(this row should be between 2 ruffles)*] across, work last sc in end of last row, turn.

Row 2: Ch 1, sc in each and in each ch across. Fasten off.

2 for 1!

Background

Row 1 (RS): Ch a multiple of 4 chs plus 1, sc in **back bar** *(see illustration on page 4)* of 2nd ch from hook, and in back bar of each ch across, turn.

Row 2: Ch 1, sc in each st across, turn.

Ruffle Layer 1

Row 1: Working in **front lps** *(see Stitch Guide)*, ch 1, (sc, dc) in first st, *sc in next st, (dc, sc) in next st, dc in front lp of next st**, (sc, dc) in next st, rep from * across, ending last rep at **, turn.

Row 2: Ch 1, sc in first st, dc in next st, [sc in next st, dc in next st] across, turn.

Row 3: Rep row 2. Fasten off.

Ruffle Layer 2

Row 1 (WS): With Ruffle upside down and WS facing and working in unworked lps of row 2 on Background, join with sc in unworked lp, dc in same st, *sc in next st, (dc, sc) in next st, dc in next st**, (sc, dc) in next st, rep from * across, ending last rep at **, turn.

Rows 2 & 3: Rep rows 2–3 of Ruffle Layer 1.

pleated ruffles

Background

Row 1 (RS): Ch a multiple of 6 chs plus 3, sc in **back bar** *(see illustration on page 4)* of 2nd ch from hook, and in back bar of each ch across, turn.

Row 2a: Working in **front lp** *(see Stitch Guide)*, ch 1, sc in each st across, turn.

Row 2b: Working in **back lps** *(see Stitch Guide)* of row 1, sc in each st across, turn.

Row 3: Ch 1, sc in first st of row 2a and 2b at the same time, sc in next st of row 2a and 2b at the same time, *sc in front lp of each of next 4 sts on row 2a, **turn,** working in unworked lps of 2a and back lps of 2b at same times, sc in each of next 4 sts, **turn**, working rem lps of row 2b, sc in each of next 4 sts, [sc in next st of row 2a and 2b at same time] twice, rep from * across, turn.

Row 4: Ch 1, sc in first st, [sc in front lp of next st, sc in back lp of next st] across to last st, sc in both lps of last st, turn.

Next row: Rep row 4 to desired length. At end of last row, fasten off.

ruffles

ruffled ruffles

Background

Row 1 (RS): Ch an odd number of chs plus 1, sc in **back bar** *(see illustrati* *on page 4)* of 2nd ch from hook, and in back bar of each ch across, turn.

Row 2: Ch 1, sc in each st across, turn.

Row 3a: Ch 1, (sc, ch 3, sc) in **front lp** *(see Stitch Guide)* of first st, [sk ne> st, (sc, ch 3, sc) in front lps of next st] across, turn.

Row 3b: Sc in each unworked lp on row 2 across, turn.

Rows 4a & 4b: Working in sts on row 3b, rep rows 3a and 3b.

Row 5: Working in sts on row 4b, ch 1, (sc, ch 3, sc) in first st, [sk next st, (sc, ch 3, sc) in next st] across. Fasten off.

ruffled waves

Background

Row 1 (RS): Ch an even number of chs plus 1, sc in **back bar** *(see illustration on page 4)* of 2nd ch from hook, and in back bar of each ch across, turn.

Row 2: Ch 1, sc in first st, [sc in **front lp** *(see Stitch Guide)* of next st, sc in **back lp** *(see Stitch Guide)* of next st] across to last st, sc in both lps of last st, turn.

Rows 3 & 4: Rep row 2.

Row 5: Ch 1, sc in first st, [sc in front lp of next st, sc in back lp of same st] across to last st, sc in both lps of last st, turn.

Rows 6 & 7: Rep row 5. At end of last row, fasten off.

triple decker

Background

Row 1 (RS): Ch multiple of 6 chs plus 2, sc in **back bar** *(see illustration on page 4)* of 2nd ch from hook, and in back bar of each ch across, turn.

Row 2: Ch 1, sc in **front lp** *(see Stitch Guide)* of each st across, turn.

Row 3: Ch 1, sc in each st across, turn.

Rows 4–7: Rep rows 2 and 3 alternately. At end of last row, fasten off.

Ruffle

Row 1: With RS facing, join with sl st in first unworked lp on row 1 of Background, sc in each lp across, turn.

Row 2: Ch 1, sc in first st, [sk next 2 sts, 5 dc in next st, sk next 2 sts, sc in next st] across, turn.

Row 3: Ch 1, sc in first st, [ch 3, sc in next st] across. Fasten off.

Rep Ruffle in unworked lps on rows 3 and 5.

smocked ruffles

SPECIAL STITCH

Back single crochet (back sc): With yarn in front of work, insert hook in st from back to front so that hook is facing down, yarn should be to right of hook, move yarn to left going under the hook, thereby catching yarn in hook, pull yarn through st turning hook counterclockwise so that hook is now facing up, yo hook from left to right and back to left catching yarn in hook, turn hook clockwise so that hook is facing down and pull through all lps on hook. This st will create an obvious vertical strand in back of work.

Background

Row 1 (RS): Ch a multiple of 8 chs plus 6, sc in **back bar** (see illustration on page 4) of 2nd ch from hook, and in back bar of each ch across, turn.

Row 2 (WS): Ch 1, **back sc** (see Special Stitch) in each st across, turn.

Row 3: Ch 1, sc in each st across, turn.

Rows 4–11: Rep rows 2 and 3 alternately. At end of last row, fasten off.

Smocking

Cut 1 strand of yarn in a manageable length. Cut more strands as needed. Strand should run under sts on WS of work to next st to be smocked.

First Column

With RS facing, working on 4th row, with tapestry needle, *counting vertical lps from left to right, pull strand from back of work to front of work at 3rd vertical lp, working vertical lps only, pull strand under 5th lp on row, [**over 5th lp then over first lp on row, under first lp** then under 5th lp] twice, rep between ** once, push strand from front of work to back of work through same st at 3rd lp, rep Smocking from * on row 8.

2nd Column

With RS facing, working on 10th row, with tapestry needle, counting vertical lps from left to right, *pull strand from back of work to front of work at 7th vertical lp, working in vertical lps only, pull strand under 9th lp on row, [**over 9th lp then over 5th lp on row, under 5th lp** then under 9th lp] twice, rep between ** once, push strand from front of work to back of work through same st at 7th lp, rep Smocking from * on row 6 and row 2. Continued working Smocking in established fashion across Background.

ruffles

subtle lattice

Post stitches are worked around
post of stitches 2 rows below
throughout.
Leave stitches behind post stitches
unworked.

Background

Row 1 (RS): With A, ch a multiple
of 8 chs plus 8, sc in **back bar** *(see
illustration on page 4)* of 2nd ch from
hook, and in back bar of each ch
across, turn.

Row 2: Ch 1, sc in each st
across, turn.

Row 3: Ch 1, sc in first st, [**fpdtr**
(see Stitch Guide) around next st, sc
in each of next 3 sts] across to last
2 sts, fpdtr around next st, sc in last
st, turn.

Row 4: Rep row 2.

Next rows: Rep rows 3 and 4
alternately. At end of last row,
fasten off.

Smocking

Cut 1 strand of B in a manageable
length. Cut more strands as needed.
Strand should run under sts on WS
of work to next st to be smocked.

First Row

With RS facing and tapestry needle,
pull strand from back of work to
front of work between first 2 fpdtr
on row 3 of Background, pull strand
under post st on right, [*over post
st on right then over post st on left,
under post st on left* then under
post st on right] twice, rep between
* once, push strand from front of
work to back of work through same st

in between the 2 post sts.
Continue working Smocking in
established fashion until all post
sts are Smocked across row 3 of
Background to last post st.

2nd Row

With RS facing and tapestry needle,
pull strand from back of work to front
of work through first st on row 5 of
Background, wrap strand around first
post st 3 times, push strand from
front of work to back of work through
same beg st.
Rep Smocking procedure as
established on First Row for each
st of 2 posts going across row 5 of
Background to last post st.
Continue working Smocking in established fashion until all post sts are
smocked.

pretty in pink baby blanket

SKILL LEVEL
INTERMEDIATE

FINISHED SIZE
34 X 40 inches

MATERIALS
- Brown Sheep Cotton Fleece light (light worsted) weight yarn (3½ oz/ 215 yds/99g per skein):
  8 skeins #CW240 pink-a-boo
- Size H/8/5mm crochet hook or size needed to obtain gauge

GAUGE
19 sts = 6 inches; 16 rows = 5 inches

PATTERN NOTES
Post stitches are worked around post of stitches 2 rows below throughout.Leave stitches behind post stitches unworked.

SPECIAL STITCH
Puff stitch (puff st): [Insert hook in indicated st, yo, pull lp through, yo] 3 times, pull last yo through all lps on hook.

INSTRUCTIONS

BLANKET
Row 1 (RS): Ch 99, sc in **back bar** *(see illustration on page 4)* of 2nd ch from hook and in back bar of each ch across, turn. *(98 sc)*

Row 2: Ch 1, **puff st** *(see Special Stitch)* in first st, ch 1, sk next st, *[puff st in next st, ch 1, sk next st] 3 times, sc in each of next 10 sts**, puff st in next st, ch 1, sk next st, rep from * across to last 8 sts, ending last rep at **, [puff st in next st, ch 1, sk next st] 3 times, puff st in next st, sc in last st, turn.

Row 3: Ch 1, sc in each of first 9 sts or chs, *[puff st, ch 1, sk next st] 4 times**, sc in each of next 10 sts, rep from * across to last 8 sts, ending last rep at **, sc in each of last 9 sts, turn.

Rows 4–9: Rep rows 2 and 3 alternately.

Row 10: Ch 1, sc in each st across, turn.

Rows 11–117: Rep rows 2–10 consecutively, ending with row 9 which is a RS row. At end of last row, **do not turn.**

Edging
Rnd 1 (RS): With RS facing and working in ends of rows, *evenly sp 117 sc across to corner, ch 2 for corner*, evenly sp 97 sc in starting ch on opposite side of row 1, ch 2 for corner, rep between * once, ch 2 for corner, evenly sp 97 sc across top, ch 2 for corner, join with sl st in beg sc, **turn.**

Rnd 2: Ch 1, sc in corner ch sp, sc in each st around with (sc, ch 2, sc) in each corner, ending with (sc, ch 2) in same ch sp as first sc, join with sl st in beg sc, turn.

Rnd 3: Ch 1, sc in corner ch sp, *[sc in next st, **fptr** *(see Stitch Guide)* around next st] across to last st before ch sp, sc in last st**, (sc, ch 2, sc) in corner ch sp, rep from * around, ending last rep at **, (sc, ch 2) in same ch sp as first sc, join with sl st in beg sc, turn.

Rnd 4: Ch 1, sc in corner ch sp, *sc in each of next 2 sts, [3 sc in next st, sc in next st] across to last st before corner, sc in last st**, (sc, ch 2, sc) in corner ch sp, rep from * around, ending last rep at **, (sc, ch 2) in same ch sp as first sc, join with sl st in beg sc, turn.

ruffles

Rnd 5: Ch 1, sc in corner ch sp, *sc in next st, fptr around next st, [sc in each of next 2 sts, 3 sc in next st, sc in next st] across to last 3 sts before corner, sc in next st, fptr around next st sc in next st**, (sc, ch 2, sc) in corner ch sp, rep from * around, ending last rep at **, (sc, ch 2) in same ch sp as first sc, join with sl st in beg sc, turn.

Rnd 6: Ch 1, sc in corner ch sp, *sc in next st, **bptr** *(see Stitch Guide)* around next st, sc in each of next 2 sts, [ch 1, sk next 5 sts, sc in next st] across to last 3 sts before corner, sc in next st, bptr around next st, sc in next st**, (sc, ch 2, sc) in corner ch sp, rep from * around, ending last rep at **, (sc, ch 2) in same ch sp as first sc, join with sl st in beg sc. Fasten off.

STITCH GUIDE

Need help? ▶ **StitchGuide.com** • ILLUSTRATED GUIDES • HOW-TO VIDEOS

STITCH ABBREVIATIONS

beg	begin/begins/beginning
bpdc	back post double crochet
bpsc	back post single crochet
bptr	back post treble crochet
CC	contrasting color
ch(s)	chain(s)
ch-	refers to chain or space previously made (i.e., ch-1 space)
ch sp(s)	chain space(s)
cl(s)	cluster(s)
cm	centimeter(s)
dc	double crochet (singular/plural)
dc dec	double crochet 2 or more stitches together, as indicated
dec	decrease/decreases/decreasing
dtr	double treble crochet
ext	extended
fpdc	front post double crochet
fpsc	front post single crochet
fptr	front post treble crochet
g	gram(s)
hdc	half double crochet
hdc dec	half double crochet 2 or more stitches together, as indicated
inc	increase/increases/increasing
lp(s)	loop(s)
MC	main color
mm	millimeter(s)
oz	ounce(s)
pc	popcorn(s)
rem	remain/remains/remaining
rep(s)	repeat(s)
rnd(s)	round(s)
RS	right side
sc	single crochet (singular/plural)
sc dec	single crochet 2 or more stitches together, as indicated
sk	skip/skipped/skipping
sl st(s)	slip stitch(es)
sp(s)	space(s)/spaced
st(s)	stitch(es)
tog	together
tr	treble crochet
trtr	triple treble
WS	wrong side
yd(s)	yard(s)
yo	yarn over

YARN CONVERSION

OUNCES TO GRAMS		GRAMS TO OUNCES	
1	28.4	25	7/8
2	56.7	40	1⅔
3	85.0	50	1¾
4	113.4	100	3½

UNITED STATES		UNITED KINGDOM
sl st (slip stitch)	=	sc (single crochet)
sc (single crochet)	=	dc (double crochet)
hdc (half double crochet)	=	htr (half treble crochet)
dc (double crochet)	=	tr (treble crochet)
tr (treble crochet)	=	dtr (double treble crochet)
dtr (double treble crochet)	=	ttr (triple treble crochet)
skip	=	miss

Single crochet decrease (sc dec): (Insert hook, yo, draw lp through) in each of the sts indicated, yo, draw through all lps on hook.

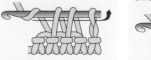

Example of 2-sc dec

Half double crochet decrease (hdc dec): (Yo, insert hook, yo, draw lp through) in each of the sts indicated, yo, draw through all lps on hook.

Example of 2-hdc dec

Reverse single crochet (reverse sc): Ch 1, sk first st, working from left to right, insert hook in next st from front to back, draw up lp on hook, yo and draw through both lps on hook.

Chain (ch): Yo, pull through lp on hook.

Single crochet (sc): Insert hook in st, yo, pull through st, yo, pull through both lps on hook.

Double crochet (dc): Yo, insert hook in st, yo, pull through st, [yo, pull through 2 lps] twice.

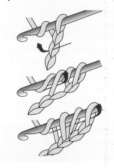

Double crochet decrease (dc dec): (Yo, insert hook, yo, draw lp through, yo, draw through 2 lps on hook) in each of the sts indicated, yo, draw through all lps on hook.

Example of 2-dc dec

Front loop (front lp) Back loop (back lp)

Front Loop   Back Loop

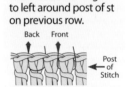

Front post stitch (fp): Back post stitch (bp): When working post st, insert hook from right to left around post of st on previous row.

Back   Front

Post of Stitch

Half double crochet (hdc): Yo, insert hook in st, yo, pull through st, yo, pull through all 3 lps on hook.

Double treble crochet (dtr): Yo 3 times, insert hook in st, yo, pull through st, [yo, pull through 2 lps] 4 times.

Slip stitch (sl st): Insert hook in st, pull through both lps on hook.

Chain color change (ch color change) Yo with new color, draw through last lp on hook.

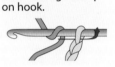

Double crochet color change (dc color change) Drop first color, yo with new color, draw through last 2 lps of st.

Treble crochet (tr): Yo twice, insert hook in st, yo, pull through st, [yo, pull through 2 lps] 3 times.

Treble crochet decrease (tr dec): Holding back last lp of each st, tr in each of the sts indicated, yo, pull through all lps on hook.

Example of 2-tr dec